ADVENTISTS IN RUSSIA

ADVENTISTS IN RUSSIA

Alf Lohne

REVIEW AND HERALD PUBLISHING ASSOCIATION
Washington, DC 20039-0555
Hagerstown, MD 21740

This book was
Edited by Raymond H. Woolsey
Designed by Richard Steadham
Cover photos by Alf Lohne and Monty S. Jacobs
Type set: 11/12 Times Roman

PRINTED IN U.S.A.

Library of Congress Cataloging in Publication Data

Lohne, Alf, 1915-
   Adventists in Russia.

   Bibliography: p. 159
   1. Seventh-day Adventists—Soviet Union.
2. Adventists—Soviet Union.   3. Soviet Union—
Church history—1917-   . I. Title.
BX6153.4.S65L65   1987   286.7'47   86-31391

ISBN 0-8280-0373-4

Contents

Introduction

Winston Churchill's nine-word description of Russia still sums up a lot of present-day realities: "A riddle wrapped in a mystery inside an enigma." No wonder that the true facts about Adventism in this huge country are hard to come by. The more I see, hear, and read about the subject, the more I liken it to Russian wooden dolls: we open one and find another smaller one inside, and another inside that, and still another and another.

I therefore conclude that it is unwise to state categorically that such and such is the situation and that all other descriptions are incorrect. So much depends on the personalities concerned, their political or religious attitudes, internal politics, and even the changing international situation. Often the eyes of the beholder determines what the person sees.

I can say that this book describes matters as my eyes saw them. It reflects my experiences while traveling extensively in most of the Soviet republics during several visits up to and including 1985. I base the story on what I noticed while worshiping with and preaching to thousands of believers, meeting individuals in dozens of homes, and in intimate discussions with ministers and laypersons. I also spent time with several government officials.

For historic facts about Seventh-day Adventists I have relied heavily on available sources, especially the archives at Adventist world headquarters in Washington, D.C. Other sources are listed when quoted.

Yet I do not claim absolute fairness in every detail. And if this book causes discussions, which I expect it to do, it may lead to a better book on the subject.

The official name of the country called Russia is the Union of Soviet Socialist Republics (U.S.S.R.). Strictly speaking, the name *Russia* refers only to the Russian Soviet Federated Socialist Republic, which indeed covers most of the country; but there are 14 other republics. The population consists of about 100 national and ethnic groups, but the Soviet Union is based mainly on the former territories of the Russian Empire. With this in mind, and according to common practice in the West, I have, for the most part, used the words Russia and Russian, and do not think this will cause misunderstandings.

—Alf Lohne

1 The Gospel Knows No Boundaries

C*hristos Voscress!"* ("Christ is risen!") With this special Russian greeting I began my Easter sermon in a Pentecostal church and later the same morning to a Baptist congregation, both in the city of Orel, a little more than 200 miles south of Moscow.

I wondered whether the audience would understand my Norwegian accent, but my suspense was short-lived. In only a fraction of a second hundreds of voices joined in the thunderous response: *"Voistinu Voscress!"* ("He is risen indeed!").

My wife and I were just as excited on this visit to the Soviet Union in 1985 as we were on any of the six earlier ones. We had boarded a train in Moscow in the evening, and since it was not one of the modern express trains, it moved slowly and made many stops along the way. It took us most of the night to reach Orel. I do not sleep well under such conditions, and I woke up every time the train stopped or started. But we enjoyed our comfortable compartment and the female conductor spared no effort to make the journey pleasant. She served us hot herbal tea and cookies and brought us all the blankets and pillows we could use.

We arrived early in the morning and wondered why our hosts scarcely allowed us time to greet the many friends who appeared at the station to welcome us. They hurried us to the hotel and made it clear that the well-provisioned breakfast table could not wait.

"Why the rush?" I protested. "It is only seven o'clock by my watch!"

"A Protestant congregation expects you to speak in 30 minutes," they said, smiling. "After that we rush to another. Later you meet with Seventh-day Adventist workers, and tonight you speak in the Adventist church!"

The appointments with Christians in other churches surprised me, but the experience turned out to be a pleasant one. I encountered no problem in establishing rapport with the congregations, who grounded their faith on a resurrected and living Saviour. That evening, visitors from both the morning appointments attended the meeting in the Adventist church. The two church pastors heartily invited me to speak in their churches any time we visit Orel again. I hope the opportunity comes!

The "Eagle" City

Founded in 1564 during the reign of Ivan the Terrible, the city of Orel proudly presents a rich historical background. The Russians built it as a fortress to fend off Tatar invaders from the Crimea. According to an old legend, when a group of Tatar warriors surrounded the fortress an eagle zoomed down out of the blue and attacked their leader. After a short, fierce fight, the eagle rose into the air only to fold its wings and drop dead into the river Oka. Badly wounded by the bird, the Tatar leader fled with all his men. When Ivan the Terrible heard the legend he named the city Orel, which means eagle. As a remembrance of this legend and their city, the Orel church presented us with a beautiful, hand-carved wooden eagle.

Nazi troops occupied Orel during World War II. Dramatic paintings in the city's war museum portray the battles fought in the surrounding region. Local guides relate stories of the heroic deeds pictured on the circular walls in one of the buildings. Visitors view paintings, tanks, guns, and other battle relics from a platform built in the center. Lifelike wax figures show soldiers in hand-to-hand combat. Everything combined

10

strongly impresses the viewer with the horrors of war.

When the Red Army liberated the city on August 5, 1943, Moscow celebrated the victory by firing a special salute. This was the first of such salutes that heralded the freeing of all the larger cities and important towns.

We gladly accepted an invitation by our local leaders to visit a monument to World War II heroes and peace. I expected to place flowers inconspicuously at the base of the monument. When we arrived, a company of uniformed young people carrying flags and banners marched forward and lined up by the monument. Then a much-decorated army officer and a woman official invited me to speak to the group. I felt they listened attentively as I shared my own memories of the war in Europe and expressed the Christian's hope and influence for peace—personal peace, peace between individuals, and peace among nations. I still do not know whether the city arranged for the youth to be there because of my visit or if it all happened by chance, but I certainly appreciated the occasion.

Visiting the "Danish Castle"

We spent one weekend in Tallinn, capital of Estonia. The local conference president, Aarne Kriisk, and the secretary-treasurer, Maimu Vali, saw to it that every hour was well utilized.

The charming old city with its historic monuments appears typically Western European in its culture and way of life. During the summer months a constant stream of tourists fills its hotels and crowds its beaches. From Finland alone an estimated 1,000 tourists a day cross the gulf to visit Tallinn.

A common cultural heritage as well as its proximity attracts Finns to the city. The Estonians, a people of Finno-Ugric stock, settled here since the first centuries after Christ. The language reflects the cultural relationship; it uses the Latin alphabet and contains many Finnish words. The name *Tallinn* comes from *taani linn* and means "Danish castle." King Waldemar II of

11

Denmark founded the city in the year 1219 after a battle on June 15. That battle influences Denmark until this day. An ancient legend tells that as King Waldemar's tired soldiers retreated before the enemy, a red flag intersected by a white cross floated down from heaven. This gave them courage to renew the fight and win the battle. The Danes adopted the red banner with its white cross as their national flag, and it still flies from Danish flagpoles.

A question-and-answer period with local Adventist pastors and evangelists proved them well grounded in denominational theology and policy. This is probably because they give serious study to the comparatively large selection of Spirit of Prophecy material available in their language.

Many of the pioneer workers in Estonia received part of their education at the Baltic Union School, which the Seventh-day Adventist Church once operated at the Suschenhof estate near Riga, on the banks of a beautiful inland lake. Opened in 1923 with 35 students, the school later expanded to accommodate 150 young people. The school administration believed in combining manual labor with theoretical studies and successfully operated a soap factory, dressmaking department, and woodworking shop in addition to its dairy and poultry farms. Most of the students earned their way by working in one of these industries. The school exerted a far-reaching influence; missionaries from Estonia went to Africa in the 1930s.

Adventists in Tallinn built their church right in the center of the busy city. The window in our modern hotel room looked out onto the church building. When we noticed people filing in through the church doors we knew it was time to leave for the meetings I was to conduct there.

Many visitors from nearby and faraway churches came in for the weekend. A male choir and other groups played an important part in the services.

Visitors enjoy the high quality of church music in this small republic, which every fifth year organizes what ranks as one of the largest song festivals in the world. A 60-acre festival ground seats 50,000 people and provides standing room for several thousand more. The huge open-air platform in front of an acoustical shell holds up to 20,000 singers. In a republic used to such performances, the quality of music presented in the Seventh-day Adventist church in the capital city measures up to its high standards.

Meeting Believers in Siberia's Far East

When Moscow police stamped our visas giving us permission to visit Khabarovsk and Irkutsk in the southeastern section of Siberia, we were delighted. In the course of several previous visits to the Soviet Union we had traveled extensively in the west and south, itinerated in central Asia, and reached as far as Novosibirsk in western Siberia. But one can understand our eagerness to visit the more remote places, where no official visitors from Adventist headquarters had visited for at least a half century. We were to be accompanied on our trip by Pastor Michael Kulakov, of whom I will speak more later.

It is a long way from Washington, D.C., to Moscow. We advanced the clock eight hours and adjusted to a new sleeping schedule. But Moscow was only the halfway point of our trip. People in New England live closer to Moscow than do those on the east coast of Russia; this gives an idea of the distances involved. When we arrived in Khabarovsk after an eight-hour night flight from the capital in a modern Soviet jet, we turned the clock forward an additional seven hours. Fortunately the Soviet airline Aeroflot does not allow smoking on domestic flights, and the stewardesses had served abundant food and nonalcoholic drinks and had made us comfortable.

The city of Khabarovsk, with its more than half million inhabitants, is situated on the Amur River. In ancient times people liked to imagine that this part of the country stood on the backs of three giant whales. In fact, the city rests upon three long hills watered by the mighty Amur, longest river in the

Soviet Union's far east. In Eastern Asia the river forms part of the border between the U.S.S.R. and the People's Republic of China. The Chinese call it the Black Dragon River.

Adventist members gave us a cordial welcome, and the local pastor, Leonid D. Rebant, and his wife extended warm hospitality. Many members, along with visitors from various other churches, had come from the city of Vladivostok, 480 miles distant, on the Sea of Japan. They all needed food, and many stayed overnight because of the vast distances they traveled. Hospitable Adventist homes opened their doors to furnish the visitors with both beds and food.

Every church here in the far east, as elsewhere in the country, seems blessed with musical talent. Many gifted young people perform in choirs and instrumental groups. They play a variety of musical instruments, including piano, violin, electric guitar, mandolin, and flute.

Baptists in Khabarovsk, who met in a hall built typically of solid Siberian logs, kindly invited Pastor Kulakov and me to speak to a packed audience at their Sunday morning service. Here also we noted many young people and listened to excellent choirs and music.

One detail from this meeting touched our hearts. Because of the tight schedule we were forced to leave before the meeting closed, in order to meet our next appointment. As the local Baptist pastor led us down the central aisle those in the audience stood to their feet and sang the Russian version of the hymn "God Be With You Till We Meet Again." As they sang they waved their handkerchiefs in farewell.

With my inner eye I still see that forest of waving hands with white handkerchiefs—an expression of fellowship with Christians we had never met before and probably will never meet again in this life. My wife and I took out our handkerchiefs to return their lovely send-off, although we felt we needed them more to dry our moist eyes.

Distant Regions Hear the Everlasting Gospel

Like most people who have never visited the far eastern part of the Soviet Union, I knew little of the vastness of the country's land mass and of the totally different nature of Siberia from the rest of the country. I had, of course, read about gold in the rivers, coal in the ground, and the abundance of minerals in the mountains—not to mention the bears in the woods and wolves on the tundra areas.

But I did not know that the world's largest and fiercest tigers roam in the endless Siberian woods. A short time before our visit five hunters caught a couple of tiger cubs, intending to send them to zoological gardens in other parts of the world. The mother tiger, however, did not permit the men to steal her babies without a fight. She stalked the hunters to their cabin, and when they inadvertently left the door open she leaped in and attacked the men. In short order she killed four of the hunters before the one survivor managed to shoot her.

To these distant regions the Advent message found its way, sometimes by unexpected means. In the city of Tobolsk, one of the chief centers of early colonization in Siberia, a man named E. Iljetsch heard about Seventh-day Adventists, but he could find none in his area. He traveled south to Turkestan and thence to Omsk, a distance of nearly 2,000 miles, in order to find an Adventist minister. There he received instruction in the truths of the three angels' messages of Revelation 14, ordered the Russian paper the Adventist Church printed at that time, and rejoicing, traveled back to his home. Back in Tobolsk he shared his newfound faith with his family and friends, some of whom gladly accepted it. Thus Adventist work began in that part of Siberia.

Both in the city of Khabarovsk on the border of Manchuria and in Irkutsk, near Mongolia, Seventh-day Adventists meet in their own buildings. Every Sabbath they study the Bible and listen to preaching from God's word. Although the church structures are humble and not located in business centers with high-rise buildings, a strong love ties the members together; nowhere else have I spoken to more attentive audiences.

In Irkutsk, on the banks of the Angara River, we spent two delightful days with Adventist workers and members. The city serves as the administrative and cultural center for eastern Siberia. In some of the gold mines located in this area miners move more gold than anywhere else in the country. Among the 600,000 inhabitants one notes many Polish names. They originate from the Polish uprising in 1863 after which the czar sent 18,600 Poles into exile in Siberia. Among the famous Russian exiles deported to this place, history records Josef Stalin and V. M. Molotov, both of whom managed to escape.

Pastor N. S. Shirokov, who lives in his privately owned log house in Irkutsk, arranged everything extremely well. Members packed the meeting place to more than capacity, and here, too, hospitality abounded. In a ceremony reserved for first visits, one of the sisters presented us, on behalf of the church, with the traditional bread and salt as a sign of special welcome.

The snowstorm that hid Lake Baikal from sight did not dampen the joy and warmth of the believers. Although the calendar indicated the middle of April and spring lurked around the corner, a coat of ice six feet thick still covered the waters of the large freshwater lake. These waters reach a depth of one mile in places. They are unmatched in the world for their clarity. The local people told me one can see a coin on the bottom, even where the lake is 40 feet deep.

Personal Witnessing

The history of the Adventist Church in Siberia—and for that matter, everywhere else in the world—shows that wherever faithful brothers and sisters in Christ settle, something happens to neighbors and friends, relatives, and companions at work. The believers may not possess all the tools and witnessing materials available to churches in other parts of the world, but the influence of Christian lives cannot be quenched. Jesus made this clear when He said, "You are the light of the world. A city set on a hill cannot be hid" (Matt. 5:14, RSV).

In 1921 I. H. Evans, president of the Far Eastern Division, visited the city of Harbin. There he found a former prima donna in the czar's opera company in Petrograd (now Leningrad) attending the Sabbath service. She once sat at the table with the czar and Emperor William II of Germany. Her fame ranked her among the great vocal soloists of Russia and Europe. As a member of the church, she now consecrated her talents to the Master to sing His praises. She told Evans she had tasted all that the world offered in wealth, dress, and applause. But while enjoying all of that, she hungered for the truth, and she testified that she never came across any people so happy and contented as the Adventists. This led her to contact the church.

The way believers' happiness in Christ attracted this woman typifies how the Adventist message reaches persons inaccessible to public preaching or to other kinds of organized church ministry. It may also reveal the way the truth will win people in places as yet untouched by the everlasting gospel.

2

A Memorable Trip

When Robert H. Pierson, president of the Seventh-day Adventist world church, asked me in 1977 to visit Adventists in the Soviet Union, I did not respond enthusiastically. In 1969, I, as secretary of the Northern European Division, and W. Duncan Eva, division president, spent about three weeks in this Communist country. Our experience during that visit did not tempt me to go back.

We found the church members cautious and afraid. Although Nikita Khrushchev no longer ruled, the antireligious campaign of 1959 to 1964 that he instigated lingered in their memories. When Adventists invited us to visit a home, they asked us not to speak English as we walked through the streets, and once inside the house, we found the windows covered so nobody could look in from the outside. It reminded me of the blackouts in Norway during World War II. After our conversations, the people left one by one. We also met under huge trees in a park, and the people arrived and left by ones and twos. They felt these precautions were prudent even though we were not discussing politics or planning to break any of the country's laws.

And I do not believe that I should take part in any secret plans when I am visiting a foreign country. I try to avoid doing anything that would create problems for the local people. But the brethren wanted to do things this way in order to prevent unnecessary suspicions or raise any questions as to the purpose of our visit. Evidently the changed conditions in the country under its new leader had not yet calmed the fears engendered during the difficult years.

On the 1969 visit, no church dared to invite us to preach when we attended Sabbath services or midweek prayer meetings. In the Moscow church one Sabbath we wrote a greeting on a piece of paper and the local pastor read it to the congregation. In another church we received permission to give greetings from the pulpit. Fortunately no time limit was fixed, and no one objected when the greeting turned out to be the longest we gave to any congregation! But our contacts were extremely limited, and when Robert Pierson asked my wife and me in 1977 to go back for another visit, I questioned the wisdom of it. Would it be worth the time and money spent? It might be just as circumscribed and frustrating as the three weeks I had spent there eight years earlier.

"Let us pray about it," Pierson said. We knelt in his office, and both of us pleaded wth the Lord for divine guidance. "I believe you should go," Pierson commented as we rose from our knees. "We need closer contact with the thousands of Adventists in the Soviet Union. In the present international climate it may also be an advantage that you have kept your Norwegian citizenship and do not carry an American passport." He outlined a plan that, I believe, opened closed doors and made the visit an unforgettable and joyful experience.

"We know your itinerary, and I promise you that every day of your trip a group of leaders will meet here and pray for you," Pierson assured me. "We will mention your names to the Lord and remind Him where you are and ask Him to give you the guidance and protection you need." In looking back, I remember how this promise encouraged us as we ourselves sought the Lord every day. We believed the promise given long ago: "Tremendous power is made available through a good man's earnest prayer" (James 5:16, Phillips). We knew that not just one "good man" but a whole group of them at world headquarters prayed for us daily.

Beginning an Uncertain Journey

I imagine that seldom, or perhaps never, has an international trip from General Conference headquarters begun with so many unknowns as the one my wife and I began on a beautiful spring day in 1977. All we had was a list with a few addresses of churches in the Soviet Union. No official central church organization existed there to prepare an itinerary and make arrangements for a profitable visit.

As is required of all tourists to the Soviet Union, we paid in advance for hotels in certain cities on certain dates, without even knowing their names and addresses. We relied on the Soviet state travel agency, Intourist, which, by the way, functioned efficiently. The agency handled all necessary reservations for travel and hotels, and representatives from Intourist met us at every stop to take care of our travel needs.

On our visa applications to the Soviet Embassy in Washington, D.C., we stated that we would travel as tourists but planned to visit Seventh-day Adventist churches and members wherever we went in the U.S.S.R. I openly stated my position as a general vice president of the world church organization. Later, when I asked the authorities for permission to speak in the churches and meet with workers, I referred to this visa request. However, we had no assurance ahead of time that we could meet with these leaders and workers or speak to members in the churches. We wondered a lot and prayed even more.

During a stopover in London on the morning of April 30, we looked up the Morning Watch text for that day. It quoted John 20:21, a prayer of Jesus for His disciples, which stated that Christ sent them into the world just as His Father had sent Him into the world. The writer of the daily devotional added this encouraging comment: ''As Christ sent forth His disciples, so today He sends forth the members of His church. The same power that the apostles had is for them. . . . He will work with them, and they shall not labor in vain!''*

We took this as a message direct from God that we needed just then, and felt very encouraged. During the following days we certainly felt that He fulfilled the promises to a degree we had not even dared to hope for. I hesitate to use superlatives such as ''the best,'' ''most exciting,'' etc., for they can become trite. But I can testify truly that the fellowship we enjoyed in talks and meetings with workers and the results we saw in this and the six succeeding visits to the Soviet Union are the brightest of all memories in our 50 years of service for the Seventh-day Adventist Church. I want to share with you some of that joy and warmth.

Leader's Faith Tried in Fire

When we arrived in London, we learned that the flight we expected to take to Moscow did not exist. We tried to contact Adventist leaders in Moscow by telephone and cable to inform them we would be arriving seven hours later than we had advised them and on a different airline, but we did not succeed in getting through. Under such circumstances we wondered whether anyone would be at the Moscow airport to meet us. At least we needed to know what hotel to go to!

We learned later that a group of Adventists had traveled hundreds of miles to welcome us with handshakes, flowers, and friendly bear hugs. They had waited at the airport for hours but finally left to catch the last train home that night. But one man had not given up. Pastor Michael P. Kulakov had checked out all other flights arriving from London that day, and faithfully watched all the passengers streaming through the arrival gates. (The enormous amount of traffic makes it easy to believe Aeroflot's claim that it is the world's largest airline, carrying 100 million passengers per year.)

What a joy to spot Pastor Kulakov's friendly face and bushy light hair among all the strangers! We learned to rely on him for most of the translation, obtaining permission to travel, making appointments with the Moscow officials, and a lot of other matters that required authority, insight, and efficient help.

The approximately 31,000 registered Seventh-day Adventists in the Soviet Union (1986 figures) have not yet been able to work out an approved Adventist constitution that spells out denominational guidelines concerning such matters as the holding of sessions, terms of office, appointment of delegates, and other administrative directives for a countrywide organization. After the church lost its administrative privileges for the country as a whole, it gradually developed a more or less official organization in most of the 15 republics that make up the Soviet Union. "Senior pastors" function as local leaders. Pastor Kulakov presides in the largest republic, which has the long and cumbersome name of Russian Soviet Federated Socialist Republic. Government authorities as well as the other senior pastors now consider him the Adventist leader for the country. He is ably assisted by N. A. Zhukaluk, eloquent speaker, warmhearted pastor, and an experienced administrator in the Ukraine, where the great majority of Seventh-day Adventists live.

Faith Tried in Fire

Kulakov comes from a solid Adventist background. His parents and grandparents belonged to the church; in fact, both his father and grandfather served as ordained ministers. In 1906 his grandfather served as an elected member of the Imperial Duma, which constituted the representative parliamentary body after the 1905 revolution. No law could be passed without its consent. When Czar Nicholas II found out that opposition candidates held the majority, he dissolved the first Duma after only 10 weeks.

While visiting in St. Petersburg (now Leningrad), Pastor Kulakov's grandfather came into contact with the Adventist message through unusual circumstances. At that time the

Adventist Publishing House in Germany printed most of the Adventist literature for Russia. The man doing the translation did not belong to the church but the Bible prophecies so impressed him that he actually went to St. Petersburg on his own to conduct a series of lectures on Daniel and Revelation. Pastor Kulakov's grandfather attended these lectures, studied on his own, and wrote to the publishing house in Germany for books on Adventist doctrines. He soon began keeping the Sabbath. Fifteen years later when an Adventist pastor came to the small village on the Don where he lived, he and his whole family joined the church through baptism.

There is a tendency in the West to assume that the only authentic Christianity in totalitarian countries is an underground movement. I do not subscribe to this. First, it is not easy to measure or evaluate spirituality. Second, we need to keep in mind that when individuals or groups in such countries make decisions we may not understand or agree with, it is often because they are forced to do it under the stress of political pressure and social change. They face stark facts and instant decisions that may affect their own welfare and that of their families. They do not, like those of us in the West, worship in popular and stately churches or relax in comfortable armchairs and theorize about what they would do in such situations.

Pastor Michael P. Kulakov, for one, has held on to his faith through experiences that testify to its dynamic quality. When he was a young minister working in Latvia during the difficult 1940s, a court sentenced him to five years in a prison camp in Siberia. His brother received the same sentence, and his father received a sentence of 10 years. Both Michael and his father survived, but his brother died during the ordeal. Yet I never heard Michael speak with bitterness about those years. Instead, he testifies to the patience he learned. He also tells how he met other prisoners who taught him English and German, both of which he now reads and speaks fluently. His knowledge of English especially opened doors to a huge treasure of theological literature and has proved invaluable in his many international contacts.

After serving his sentence in prison, Kulakov was exiled for life to Kazakhstan, where he worked for 20 years, building up the members' faith in the Bible and its message. He even found time to teach himself Greek and Hebrew. He hopes someday to complete a much-needed translation of the Bible into modern Russian. He wants to show the authorities that the Adventist faith does not make people into enemies of the state but into loyal citizens who want to practice their faith and live in peace.

The six children he and his wife, Anna, reared—three sons and three daughters—all accepted the faith of their parents, grandparents, and great-grandparents. Such results come not only from what the children heard preached from the pulpit but from the genuine Christianity practiced in the close confines of the family circle. This shows stalwart qualities that outsiders can hardly understand but might well envy.

Michael and Anna firmly believe that divine guidance brought them together. She, too, grew up in a staunch Adventist family that respected the Word of God and practiced regular attendance at Sabbath services. She naturally made the decision to accept Christ and follow in His footsteps. In the small church she belonged to, she was the only young woman. For her to find a young man of the same faith seemed an impossibility. But one night she dreamed about her future and heard a voice say that her husband's name would be Kulakov. It so happened that Michael was exiled to the area where Anna lived, and, of course, a happy wedding ceremony soon took place. He still marvels about her willingness to cast her lot with that of a poor exile!

The Kulakov family now lives in Tula, a city about 110 miles south of Moscow, with a population of about 600,000. Nearby, the great writer Leo Tolstoy owned a beautiful estate. Kept just as when the count lived there, the house gives the visitor the feeling that he might appear at any moment. I noticed on my visit that his library included books in the more than a dozen languages he mastered.

In Tula we saw a new and attractive Adventist church building under construction, replacing a wooden building that could no longer house the growing congregation. This probably sounds strange to Westerners, who usually hear only of churches being torn down and closed. Construction began after the authorities granted permission to build and the necessary preparations were finished. Generous gifts from the members and donations from other churches within the country paid for all the materials used. Everything from the drawing of the plans, the laying of the foundation, and the construction of the building to the interior decoration was done by members themselves.

With guidance of local craftsmen, 15 young men from other churches helped erect the building. They worked enthusiastically, not only because they wanted to support the church but also because they took advantage of the association with pastors of experience to further their preparation for the ministry. Intense studies filled their spare time. At the dedication Dr. Pierre Lanares, from Switzerland, served as guest speaker. The state holds the deed to the building, but the local congregation uses it and takes the responsibility for its upkeep. No fixed contributions can be exacted from individuals, but freewill offerings cover all the expenses.

Fabulous Moscow

At some point in their trip most visitors to the Soviet Union arrive in Moscow, and so did we. This capital city of the largest country in the world impresses visitors in many ways. Its 8,546,000 inhabitants live in a city spread out over 1,023 square miles. During our several visits we received good service, especially in the gigantic Hotel Rossiya. With its capacity to house 6,000 guests in 3,200 rooms, it tops the list of large hotels in Europe and no doubt is among the largest in the world. We found it easy to get lost in the building's maze of floors and hallways, especially if we happened to enter the hotel by a different entrance from the one we exited! Its concert hall, in the center of the courtyard, seats 3,000 people. One can dine in any of 32 restaurants and eating places. Because of its position in the heart of Moscow—on the edge of Red Square and within walking distance of the Baptist church on Pokrovsky Boulevard, where the Adventists worship on Wednesday evenings and Sabbath mornings—we appreciated the fact that the Russian leaders lodged us here. The Baptists use it the other days of the week.

From our hotel window we viewed the red star above the Kremlin and heard the Kremlin bells. A few hundred yards away people streamed in and out of GUM, the huge department store that tour guides say can handle 20,000 customers at once. Nearby the famous jewel of Russian architecture, St. Basil's Cathedral, attracts thousands of national and foreign tourists. Local residents told us an old story about it, the truth of which I cannot prove. According to the legend, Ivan the Terrible built the church to commemorate the conquest of Kazan. He asked the architect if he could build another church more beautiful than St. Basil's. When the architect said he could, Ivan ordered his eyes put out with a poker.

Lenin's mausoleum, also located on Red Square, is open to visitors on certain days of the week. And in the burning heat of summer and the freezing cold of winter the waiting line stretches across Red Square and winds through the park along the Kremlin's walls. Tourists, Muscovites, and whole families from the countryside wait up to four hours to get inside the tomb, which is made of rose-colored granite.

It is an extraordinary experience to walk by the black velvet-covered platform where Lenin lies, dressed in a black suit, white shirt, and black tie. The crowd files past silently, closely watched by guards armed with guns and fixed bayonets. They immediately hush into silence anyone who tries to talk or even whisper. Noting the reverence with which the people pass, one gets the impression that the honor shown the founder of this Communist country borders on religious worship, at least on the part of some. Some weep and all seem awed.

From 1953 to 1961 the bodies of Lenin and Stalin lay side by side on the platform, and both names adorned the exterior of the mausoleum. But one night workers erased Stalin's name and removed his body to a small plot behind the mausoleum near the Kremlin wall. A small slab on the grass bears his name.

The citadel of the Kremlin is one of the city's greatest sights. Entering through Spassky Gate, one comes upon 90 acres of ancient churches, palaces, and museums with breathtaking exhibitions. The cover on a Bible contains nearly 57 pounds of gold and a cupful of tear-shaped emeralds. The 2,000 precious gems decorating a throne represent immense value. A French jeweler said that if he should appraise the value of the treasures within the Kremlin walls he would start at $1 billion (American). And he saw only one third of the rooms. No wonder that this wild extravagance on the part of Russia's rulers enraged a population that for the most part lived in squalid poverty.

Just inside the gate we noted the huge bronze cannon called Czar Puchka. Sixteen feet in length and weighing 40 tons, nothing like it exists anywhere in the world. Nobody ever dared to fire it for fear it would explode. Nearby stands the largest bell in the world, Tsar Kolokol. It weighs 200 tons. When construction workers hoisted it up into place, it fell and an 11-ton piece broke off as it hit the ground. It now sits where it fell, the bell that never rang beside the cannon that never fired.

For me, however, time did not allow for extended sightseeing. Impressive museums, great art galleries, famous concert halls, scientific exhibitions, and architectural wonders of the past and present were just too many. We always hoped to see them on the next trip.

A visit with the officials of the Council on Religious Affairs headed our list of important appointments. This committee was appointed in 1966 to deal with all church-state matters. The Council for the Affairs of the Russian Orthodox Church had operated in a similar capacity since 1943. The Council on Religious Affairs implements the policies of the Communist Party and sees to it that local authorities neither go beyond their instructions with regard to the churches, nor neglect them. It is also the secular organization to which the churches must refer such questions as the opening or closing of churches, disputes with local authorities, and the holding of church conferences. Much of my time and work in the Soviet Union would depend on the decisions and recommendations made by this powerful ministry. Remembering my praying colleagues at headquarters helped me to prepare for my first meeting with the council in an optimistic spirit.

3

Celebrating
Spiritual Feasts

After a cordial welcome in their central office, the leading officials in the Ministry of Religious Affairs allotted us all the time we needed. I soon discovered that E. A. Tarasov, department head in the council, knows quite a bit about Adventist doctrines and practices. He has attended several Adventist churches and knows many Adventist ministers by name. We frankly discussed matters of mutual concern and interest.

I tried to present a true picture of the Adventist attitude toward state regulations and the relationship of the world church to national Adventist organizations. Other questions of interest were a proposed visit by R. H. Pierson to the Soviet Union, sending delegates to General Conference sessions, and permitting young men to study at church colleges abroad. At present no Adventist school of any kind operates in Russia.

I am glad to say that these requests received an affirmative reply. Pierson did visit the Soviet Union as an official guest of the church the following year, and his successor Neal C. Wilson, visited on the same basis soon after he took office. Both visits excited and delighted Adventist members and did much to promote an increased understanding between two factions in the church in Russia. Two young men received permission to study at Newbold College, and several others at the Friedensau Theological Seminary in the German Democratic Republic. Small groups of delegates from the Soviet Union attended the

General Conference sessions in Vienna, Dallas, and New Orleans. Two of the leaders, Kulakov and Zhukaluk serve as members of the General Conference Executive Committee and attend the Annual Council each October.

We gained a good insight into the laws and regulations of the country by listening to the officials explain how the authorities apply them. During successive visits to the country over the past decade I met with these same officials in Moscow and also with local authorities in several of the 15 republics. Naturally, atheists and Christians cannot agree on everything, but face-to-face meetings and frank statements of opinions promote a better understanding. Where misunderstandings may exist, personal contact smooths the way not only for politicians and statesmen but also for religious leaders and national authorities.

To illustrate the friendly atmosphere during such meetings, let me give a detail or two from the conversations. Once an official asked me my father's first name. "Edward," I answered. He smiled, "Well, from now on we will call you Edwardovich!" He then turned to my wife and asked for her father's name. When she told him "Enoch" he said, "Then from now on we will not call her Mrs. Lohne, but Enochovna!" This is the way Russians on friendly terms address one another.

On another occasion I asked one of the men: "Do you know what I would do if I were Mr. Brezhnev?" (Leonid Brezhnev was then secretary of the Communist Party and the undisputed ruler.) When he looked at me questioningly I went on: "I would try to make a Seventh-day Adventist out of every person in the Soviet Union!"

"Why?" he asked.

"Because they make such good citizens," I replied. "They believe in the Bible teaching that all Christians should be subject to the authorities as long as they can serve their Lord according to His Holy Word. They work conscientiously because they do not drink alcohol. You can trust them. They will not steal, because their religion demands honesty. Yes, I would try to make everyone a good Seventh-day Adventist!''

He probably understood me to mean people should be converted by force. This is what Prince Vladimir I of Kiev did in the year 988 when he brought Russia into the fold of Greek Orthodox Christianity. He forced the people to throw their heathen gods into the Dniepr River and ordered them into the water for baptism. And into the water they went by the thousands. The main thoroughfare of Kiev, through which, according to tradition, Vladimir led the people to be baptized, still bears the name Kreshnatik, meaning ''street of baptism.'' Probably this friendly gentleman with whom I conversed a thousand years later thought of this when he said: ''No, you cannot make everyone Adventists; you see, we have religious liberty in this country!''

Historic Meeting in Moscow

At that first meeting with the representatives of the Council for Religious Affairs in Moscow, I received permission to preach in Adventist churches in several cities. I did not know then what a thrilling experience was in store for me.

In Moscow, Adventists normally meet in the Baptist church building on a side street off Pokrovsky Boulevard only on Wednesday for prayer meeting and on Sabbath morning for two services. But the Baptists kindly canceled their Friday night choir practice so that we could meet an extra night that week. How the church leaders got word to the members about this extra meeting, I do not know. They cannot advertise in the newspapers, and comparatively few own telephones. But at the time appointed, believers filled the 500-seat church. Evidently they know how to communicate with one another in this great metropolis.

Next morning the attendance was simply overwhelming. There were no empty seats; people packed every inch of standing room. Never before had so many Adventists crammed this venerable house of prayer. During the preceding 24 hours they had boarded airplanes, trains, buses, and private cars to make their way to Moscow. They came from nearby cities and villages, from faraway Siberia, Moldavia, Estonia, the Ukraine, and other republics. One Adventist, who had grown up in the message and was well acquainted with church history, wrote a letter, quoted in *Adventist Review,* as follows:

"Without exaggeration I can say that this visit is a true historical event in the life of our church here. Adventists have never before had such large meetings as have taken place during these weeks. Our guests from the General Conference saw with their own eyes the thousands of members who attended the regular and special meetings. They were greeted with unspeakable joy by members and ministers from neighboring and sometimes very distant churches (as far away as 2,500 miles) who came to the services. And those who came thanked God for the fresh current of air that was brought into our churches." [1]

Why this great interest? One thing we know for sure—they did not come because they expected to hear a fluent speaker. This was the first time I preached to any audience in the Soviet Union, so they did not know what kind of sermons to expect. Besides, church administrators, unlike popular evangelists, usually are not noted for their eloquence as speakers! I believe their enthusiasm stemmed from another and more important source.

In her autobiography, *My Life,* Golda Meir relates her experience in Moscow when in 1948 she began her work as Israel's first ambassador to the Soviet Union. A few weeks after her arrival she went to the synagogue to celebrate Rosh Hashanah, the Jewish New Year. She describes the huge crowds that turned out to see her. Pictures taken at the time show the streets around the synagogue filled with several thousand Jews. They came because they knew Golda Meir would be there. But she realized she as a person was not the great attraction. It was what she represented that caused the stir and awakened interest. She wrote, ''Of course, I knew that they would have showered the same love and pride on a broomstick if it had been sent to them to represent Israel.'' [2]

Similarly, the great attendance at the Adventist meetings was not because of my wife and me as persons. But this was the first visit in about half a century of a General Conference officer, voted by the General Conference Executive Committee and with official permission from state authorities to openly represent the Adventist world organization. As loyal Soviet citizens, they love their country and honor and respect its laws. They are also faithful Christian believers with great respect for the divine teachings of the Bible, and they have a high regard for the General Conference. To them we were not just regular visitors among many. We represented the church they love, the church that unites them with a Christian family that has members among all nations around the globe. What a thrill to meet thousands of lovely people and share the bread of life with them during three weeks of joyful fellowship.

I believe that those currently in positions of authority in Russia understand the Adventist position. We do not aim at changing political systems. Our mission is to proclaim the message of salvation, which changes lives and makes men, women, and youth an influence for good. In this way we try to make the world a better place. Adventists live as loyal citizens of whatever country they belong to. We do not believe that an open relationship means compromising one's faith. In all countries we inform the authorities of our position in a polite way and leave the consequences to God.

Unforgettable Experiences

While preaching in Moscow, I noticed many tape recorders in use. Several microphones dangled from the balcony. When I finished speaking, clicks resounded from all around the sanctuary as listeners turned off their recorders. I learned later that the recorded tapes reached the farthest corners of the Soviet Union within a short time. For instance, when we arrived in Alma-Ata near the Chinese border a few days later, a woman outside the church greeted me in German: "I am so glad you have come here! I have just listened to the sermons you preached in Moscow two weeks ago, and I want to hear more." That is why I dared not repeat sermons while visiting in Russia!

On this visit we traveled thousands of miles by air inside the Soviet Union. An impessive armada of Aeroflot airplanes covers this huge country with a network of routes to its farthest points. Air travel is inexpensive, and many people use the airline. Every plane we traveled on carried a full load. The airline treats foreigners as special guests. Aeroflot's representatives met us at each airport we used. Except in Tallinn, Estonia, they led us into special rooms or buildings for foreigners. Often they escorted us to our seats in the airplane ahead of all the other passengers, and upon arrival at our destination let us leave the plane first. They make inflight announcements in Russian only, but the stewardesses are quick to offer help when needed, as we discovered when my wife suffered a bout of air sickness.

Church members everywhere showed an eagerness to greet us. We remember fondly our reception in one city. Since we arrived there by train about midnight, accompanied by several pastors, we did not expect anyone to meet us. What a surprise to see a group of people waiting with flowers on the platform! I immediately removed my glasses from my breast pocket where I usually keep them. By this time I knew by experience that the welcome would include hearty Russian bear hugs as well as warm smiles, handshakes, and flowers. I thought it enough to risk my ribs, but not also my glasses!

The group of about 20 standing on the platform here in the middle of the night was just the beginning. When we walked up to the station I saw a sight unique in all my travels around the world. Hundreds of members from Adventist churches in the area, waited in two lines to welcome us. First stood the members of a large choir, the women dressed in white blouses and black skirts and the men in white shirts and black trousers. As we walked between the two lines members thrust bright bouquets of flowers into our arms. Most touching of all among the tulips, lilacs, carnations, and roses, we noted flowers that quite evidently had been cut from flowerpots in private homes. Before going to bed that night, we filled all the vases the hotel could provide. The rest we put into the bathtub.

Afterward we heard of a stranger in town who marveled at all the people, the flowers, and the welcome. He approached an Adventist woman and asked the reason for the celebration. "We are welcoming a brother and a sister," was the answer. His reply describes the ties that bind Adventists together: "You must belong to a very large family!"

The next day a full program occupied every hour, from early morning until late at night. We saw monuments and relics depicting the city's heroic resistance to invaders during World War II. The officials at the local office of Religious Affairs told us they had granted permission to remodel the Adventist church and greatly increase its seating capacity. The church members could now continue to gather materials for the project. At the evening meeting we saw the need for such an expansion. Again so many people came that a large part of the audience stood outside and listened through loudspeakers. A large brass band, which would have taken up much space inside, assembled in the yard and played numbers under the open windows. Never before did we see special music for the church service presented from outside!

4

God Leads
in Mysterious Ways

I believe that when all those who sleep in their graves hear God's voice and come out (John 5:28, 29), Catherine II, empress of Russia from 1762 to 1796, will be surprised at the results of one of her actions. She will discover that the colonization of Alaska and the increase of Russia's control over the Baltic areas and the Ukraine were not her greatest contributions to the Russian people. Neither are the partitioning of Poland, annexing the Crimea, or seizing control of the northern coast of the Black Sea her greatest achievements.

Her political skill and enthusiastic patronage of literature, education, and the fine arts, along with her own literary productions, gave her a glorious reputation among her contemporaries, who believed she merited the title of Catherine the Great. She carried on an extensive correspondence with one of her admirers, Voltaire (1694-1778), French philosopher and historian. He reached great literary and intellectual heights, and some consider him to be the personification of the eighteenth-century Age of Enlightenment in Europe. But all this shed only a transient glory on the mighty Russian czarina.

Most popular history books mention only in passing, if at all, Catherine's special act that brought such significant results for God's people. During her reign, the common people, especially the peasants, suffered as much as they had under previous rulers, while she and the aristocracy reveled in luxury. At a certain point God used the czarina as a tool in His hand to

39

prepare the way for tens of thousands in Russia to accept God's last message to the world. But, God indeed leads in mysterious ways. He could even use an empress whose private life was far from exemplary and whose government left much to be desired.

No ruler or despot can thwart God's will, for "the Lord controls the mind of a king as easily as he directs the course of a stream" (Prov. 21:1, TEV). The ungodly ruler Pilate thought himself a great man of power when he said to Jesus, "Remember, I have authority to set you free and also to have you crucified" (John 19:10, TEV). But Jesus brought him down to size when He answered, "You have authority over me only because it is given to you by God" (verse 11, TEV).

From our vantage point in history it is easy to recognize Catherine the Great's invitation to the Mennonites to settle in southern Russia as the first stepping-stone for the entrance of the Adventist message into that great country. The fact that the process moved slowly, taking more than a hundred years and involving people of other nationalities in faraway places, in no way diminishes the importance of her action. But when she issued the invitation, neither she nor anyone else imagined such consequences.

Born in Germany to Prince Christian August of Anhalt-Zerbst, Catherine became the first and only German ever to occupy the imperial throne of Russia. In spite of her personal weaknesses and mistakes as an empress, no one questions her love for her adopted country and her desire to make Russia prosperous and powerful. Part of this effort was directed to the development of the vast uncultivated areas in southern Russia. Probably her German background led her to think of the extremely industrious and successful Mennonite farmers who because of religious intolerance and persecution in the Netherlands and Switzerland had emigrated to Prussia.

Numerous experiences in Mennonite history testify to their readiness to endure any inconvenience or even suffering rather than give in to pressure or deny their faith. One of their pioneers in Germany, a former Benedictine monk named Michael Sattler, wrote out the basic theology of the Swiss Anabaptists, the movement that spawned the Mennonites. Dr. J. C. Wenger, professor of historical theology in Goshen Biblical Seminary, a school of the Associate Mennonite Biblical Seminaries, describes Sattler's fate as follows:

"Catholic leaders in South Germany did not accept the teaching and writing of this former monk. So they had him put in prison in Binzdorf. After 11 weeks, he and some other Anabaptists were taken to Rottenburg for trial and execution. Sattler was, of course, considered the chief heretic, and nine charges were placed against him:

"1. That he had disobeyed the Imperial Mandate (he denied it).

"2. That he rejected the magical power of the bread and wine—transubstantiation (he admitted this).

"3. That he said infant baptism does not save (he admitted this charge).

"4. That he rejected extreme unction—the anointing of the sick to prepare them for death (he claimed it was not what James taught).

"5. That he despised Mary, mother of god (he claimed not to despise her but rejected the idea that she can mediate between God and man).

"6. That he opposed the swearing of oaths (he admitted this).

"7. That he advocated eating the bread and wine, mixed, from a plate, in the Lord's Supper (no reply recorded).

"8. That he violated his monastic vow and married a wife (he claimed the New Testament gave him permission to do this).

"9. That he had said that if a Turkish invasion took place, and if he had to fight, he would prefer to fight on the side of the Turks (to this rather radical and rash charge he pleaded guilty, saying that the Turks did not know any better! But Christians who go to war are Turks in spirit).

"By the end of the trial, the clerk of the court was very angry. He declared that to execute Sattler with a sword would be a service to God. The 24 judges filed out and soon returned with a horrible sentence: Sattler's tongue was to be cut off. His body was to be repeatedly wounded with red-hot pincers. And finally, he was to be burned at the stake. This sentence was carried out on or about May 20, 1527. His courageous wife followed him to a martyr's death a few days later." [1]

The Mennonites enjoyed religious freedom in Prussia for a time, but things changed. The following incident is typical of the difficulties that made life intolerable in their adopted homeland.

Frederick William I, king of Prussia, "maintained a palace guard of giants, whom he proudly called his *sieben fussler* (seven footers). One day the king's recruiting agents, passing through the Mennonite community of Tilsit, saw several likely candidates for Frederick's special service, and took the unwilling and protesting stalwarts to Potsdam. The church elders quickly reminded the king of the special exemption his predecessors had guaranteed them. The young men were released, but Frederick in anger ordered those of the Tilsit settlement to leave his realm forever. The majority found refuge in Polish Prussia (see *Mennonite Encyclopedia,* Vol. II, p. 386)." [2]

When political powers partitioned Poland in 1772 to 1795, they assigned the northern part to Prussia, and once again the Mennonites faced the problems from which they fled. This caused them to look for asylum where they could worship God and follow their religious beliefs according to their convictions.

Mennonites Accept Russia's Invitation

Soon after taking power, Catherine II issued decrees of toleration, in 1762 and 1763. These encouraged Europeans seeking religious freedom to settle in Russia's newly acquired territories in the south. The Mennonite settlers in Danzig, then under Prussian rule, eagerly studied the invitation from the empress. The privileges she promised were within the framework of a *Privilegium* granted by the Russian government. It guaranteed each family perpetual possession of 65 dessiatines (about 165 acres) of land and the right to future industrial expansion. Further, the family would receive a loan of 500 rubles as support until the first harvest was in, free use of the crown's forest, and tax exemption for 10 years. The government would also exempt them from all civil and military service. They could enjoy religious freedom for themselves, but laws forbade them to seek converts among orthodox Russians. No laws restricted religious proselyting among the Muhammadan population.[3]

The permission to evangelize only the Muhammadans did not limit the Mennonites much as it might seem. The religion of Islam counted more adherents in the Soviet Union than any other except the Orthodox Church. (It still does. Although not all practice their religion strictly, several sources estimate that between 30 and 50 million people in Russia consider themselves Muslims. Only four countries in the world—Indonesia, Pakistan, India, and Bangladesh—have a greater Muslim population).

Naturally, the invitation from Russia interested the oppressed Mennonites of Danzig. They sent two representatives to Petrograd; they met with Catherine herself and heard the promises confirmed. In 1789 more than 200 Mennonite families founded their first colony on Chortitza, a long, narrow, previously uninhabited island in the river Dnieper in the Ukraine. For these pioneers the raising of livestock emerged as the best means of livelihood, sheep breeding predominating. Soon the settlement boasted a flock of one thousand sheep.

Upon the death of Catherine II, her son, Paul I, took the imperial throne. He repeated in writing the privileges granted by his mother to the settlers in southern Russia. This caused a renewed emigration wave of Mennonites from western Prussia. They left partly as a protest against the established social system, which favored the wealthy, and partly because of the militaristic attitude of the government, which threatened their pacifist beliefs. The renewed invitation from Russia opened for them new vistas of freedom, peace, and prosperity. Soon a second colony, on the Molochnaya River near the Sea of Azov, counted about 1,200 families. This place is situated in what is now the Zaparozhe province of the Ukraine. Eventually the immigrants established more than 50 widely separated colonies.

Catherine's interest in agriculture led to unique projects. In 1765 she founded what she called the "Free Econonic Society for the Encouragement in Russia of Agriculture and Household Management." Two years later she offered 1,000 gold pieces for the best set of recommendations on how to organize an agricultural economy "for the common good." This Europe-wide contest received 164 entries, the prize-winning essay coming from France.[4]

The invitation to the agriculturally skilled German pietists probably produced the best results of all Catherine's efforts to improve agriculture, develop virgin lands and introduce new farming methods to the country. A growing demand for Russian wheat in western Europe in the 1850s provided a strong incentive for the Mennonite farmers to increase production. The mechanization of agriculture became a necessity and resulted in the Mennonite farm machinery industry. Before World War I, eight Mennonite factories produced 10 percent of all agricultural machinery in south Russia. It is said that the quality was fully equal to their counterparts from North America.[5] And the Mennonites became well known as master farmers.

Moving to the New World

But once again the situation changed for the Mennonites. In the 1870s Czar Alexander II issued a decree introducing universal military conscription into Russia. Then the special privileges giving the Mennonites exemption from military service would end. Intense negotiations with the authorities in St. Petersburg led to a decree in 1875 that provided for all Mennonites in Russia an obligatory forestry service in place of serving in the military. Evidently the czar did not want these valuable subjects to leave the country. But this decree came too late; conservative believers feared that even obligatory state service would violate their historic position on peace. They were also aware of the coming Russification program whereby the government would take over their schools and force them to use the Russian language in place of German. Therefore, by 1873 emigration to Canada and the United States already was under way. Soon 18,000 Mennonites emigrated. Canada offered them two reserves, and large numbers settled in Kansas and Nebraska. They "left Russia without ill-will," however, and "sent an address of thanks to the government of the czar expressing appreciation for the good they had received" there.[6]

Before leaving Russia, the Mennonites wanted to find out what to expect in their future home. They read in the Bible that Moses picked 12 men from the different tribes and sent them into Canaan with specific instructions "to explore the land. . . . Find out whether the soil is fertile and whether the land is wooded. And be sure to bring back some of the fruit that grows there" (Num. 13:16-20 TEV). Likewise, the Mennonites selected 12 qualified men from their different settlements and sent them to Canada and the United States to learn about the conditions that would affect their religious freedom and livelihood. The good report they brought cleared the way for the emigration to start within a few weeks of their return.

The following report shows the good reputation these immigrants enjoyed in American political circles:

"A petition was presented in the lower house of Congress (December, 1873) relative to setting aside large tracts of public land for establishing large, compact Mennonite communities.

A senator from Minnesota said that unless Congress wished to drive away 40,000 of the best farmers in Russia and have them choose to settle in Canada instead, they would vote passage of the bill.

"A senator from Pennsylvania told of the Mennonites in his state who were exemplary citizens, maintaining the best schools in the land. One of Indiana's senators told of a book he had that described the persecution they had borne, their unwillingness to carry arms, and their honest charitable spirit.

"A senator from Connecticut hinted that the Mennonites might not make good citizens because of their refusal to fight. In reply, a senator from Nebraska said, 'Have we not enough of the fighting elements in America? . . . if there is any portion of the world that can send us a few advocates of peace, in God's name, let us bid them welcome. We want citizens of that kind. They can make our nation great.'

"Although the petition finally miscarried, congressional debates were indicative of the high regard for the prospective immigrants from Russia.

"Representatives of government and of railroad companies were not slow in providing transportation and other conveniences. The agents were aware that the bearded men in drab-colored suits and broad-brimmed hats represented some of the most industrious and prosperous farmers of Europe." [7]

Another author writes just as positively about the abilities and industry of the descendants of these welcome immigrants:

"Now, when these Mennonites moved to Kansas, they perpetuated their gentle traditions . . . continued their unassuming lives . . . grew wheat in their own special way from their own special seed.

"Then came the big drought. The worst in years. It was so bad that the Department of Agriculture sent an expert from Washington to examine the withered crops. And it must have been a barren sight . . . acre upon acre of parched Kansas prairie.

"Then the government inspector came to the Mennonites' land. What he found started a revolution on the plains. While others' wheat failed . . . had been starved and blistered by the drought . . . the Mennonites' wheat was thriving, reaching bravely for the killer sun!

"In Kansas today, the Mennonite strain of wheat seed is still being used. So hearty is this strain that it can be planted in the fall and harvested in the spring, actually resisting 'winter kill.' Needless to say, drought continues to be a small obstacle for Mennonite wheat to overcome."

The author even adds the speculation that if the Mennonites had not felt forced by the czarist government to leave Russia, today "the United States, instead of selling, might be buying wheat from the Russians!" [8]

One story as to how this hard wheat came to America has survived through the years. It tells about a little girl immigrating from the Crimea with her parents, who brought a handful of grain tied into a corner of her apron.

In their new surroundings some of the settlers picked up religious ideas and convictions that would find their way back to Russia and eventually affect tens of thousands of people there. The Mennonite move *out* of Russia brought Seventh-day Adventists *into* Russia, as one of the ultimate results of Catherine's decrees of 1762 to 1763 began to crystallize.

5 An Unlikely Missionary

Jacob Reiswig and his Lutheran parents came to the United States with the immigrants who arrived from Russia in 1875. One Sunday a couple of years later, Jacob and his family, on their way home from attending a service in the primitive sod building that served as a church, picked up a young man in their one-horse carriage. Since he could not fit inside the carriage, the man had to ride standing on the rear axle. When he heard they had attended a religious meeting, he began to talk to them about Bible subjects. Jacob became so interested that he invited the young man to their home for further discussion.

In spite of the fact that Jacob spoke very little English and their guest spoke no German, they managed to communicate and study together until early morning. Before he left, the visitor gave Jacob a German tract, "Warum Nicht Früher Endeckt?" ("Why Not Discovered Before?"). It dealt with the subject of the seventh-day Sabbath. Jacob studied it carefully and became convinced that the seventh day of the week, Saturday, is the Sabbath according to Bible teaching. At the next week's Sunday meeting in the sod church, he presented this view, and before long the entire group met regularly on the seventh day of the week.[1]

These new believers had friends and relatives among the Baptists and Mennonites who had stayed behind in Russia, and now they began sending them tracts and papers dealing with the new light they discovered in the Bible. One tract, with the title "The Third Angel's Message," came into the hands of a member of the Church of the Brethren in a village in southern Russia. He considered it dangerous heresy that might lead earnest members of his church astray, so he hid it in his house for three years. One day, however, he told a fellow church member his secret. His friend was Gerhard Perk, 23 years old. At the General Conference session of 1909 Gerhard told what happened next:

"This made me curious. I thought perhaps these publications might have some connection with the great temptation, or falling away, when antichrist was to be revealed. I asked my neighbor to let me have this literature, that I might read it in secret. For a long time he refused, but finally he consented, and let me have it, after I had promised not to allow anyone else to read it.

"I took the publication, and went into the haymow and read it through three times; then I copied the address given on the tract. I was at once convinced that the tract I had read was the truth; but I dared not say anything about it to my neighbors.

"The same year, I became a worker for the British and Foreign Bible Society. I also ordered some publications from America on the third angel's message, and Brother A. Kunz sent these, and began correspondence with me. I was soon afterward sent from Moscow to Siberia to scatter Bibles in that region. It was while in Siberia that I began keeping the Sabbath. It was very hard for me to begin alone, contrary to the wishes of my father and mother, and against the tide of public opinion." [2]

God's Leading Hand

As he traveled and sold Bibles in Siberia, Perk went through an experience that convinced him of God's guiding hand in his life and gave him the courage to obey Him in all things. He planned to work in the Siberian city of Irbit, where many Europeans attended an annual fair that lasted four weeks. He hoped to sell many Bibles there, so he sent ahead a good supply, worth about $1,000. When he arrived in Irbit he found, to his disappointment, that the Bibles had not arrived. For four weeks he inquired and searched for them in vain. Things looked dark for Perk. The fair closed, so a great opportunity for sales no longer existed. The loss of the Bibles would be a financial disaster. Worst of all, he might lose his job as a Bible colporteur of the British and Foreign Bible Society. Perk decided to seek the Lord in a special way. He says:

"Finally, I resorted to fasting and prayer. For three days I neither ate nor drank. On the third day the Lord heard my prayer and helped me find my books. It was said that the one who had been transportating them was slain, and that the books had been hidden in the woods. Wonderful to relate, after receiving these books, I was only one day in disposing of them all." [3]

He describes how he sold them. He stopped at a huge railway factory that employed more than 10,000 workers. *Here is my opportunity,* he thought, and he went straight to the manager and asked permission to sell his books to the workers.

"Nothing doing," the manager replied. His negative attitude seemed to close the doors. But Perk did not take no for an answer. He went to his lodging and wrote a letter to the manager, explaining that his books contained power to make men better, especially to keep them from drinking. Perk received permission to canvass right in the factory.

Never before had he sold Bibles so rapidly. A man was assigned to help him and took him through the factory, notebook and pencil in hand, introducing him to the workers. At first Perk attempted to explain the content of the Bible and what it could do for its readers but his helper said, "Do not take so much time. They will have to pay for the book anyway." [4] He then wrote down name after name.

The experience affected Perk deeply. He testifies: "This experience gave me courage to begin keeping the Sabbath, and from that time on I have observed the seventh day. The Lord gave me power to perserve in this, when standing alone.'' [5]

Thus, Gerhard Perk, a young man born into a Mennonite settlement in south Russia, found his way to the Seventh-day Adventist Church. At the General Conference session he spoke through a translator:

"I am very happy in the privilege of being one of the first to become a Seventh-day Adventist in Russia. I do not know whether I was the very first believer in that country or not; I have never learned of anyone accepting the truth there before I accepted it." [6]

His knowledge of the Russian and German languages made it possible for him to give valuable service as a translator for German-speaking Adventist workers who later went to Russia.

An Unlikely Missionary

When L. R. Conradi organized the first German church in the United States among the Russian immigrants, he noted the burden they felt for the land and people they had left behind. They were not satisfied with just sending literature, although that was important enough. Conradi described how an unlikely missionary volunteered:

"One old gentleman . . . stepped up—a good, faithful brother—and said, 'Brethren, I would like to go to Russia.'

" 'Go to Russia! What for?'

" 'To do missionary work.'

" 'Why, he can't talk [he had a speech defect]; it would be better for him to settle down.'

" 'He is too old to go there.' " [7]

The members in his church who knew him tried to persuade him not to go, because of his age, his stuttering speech, and lack of money. But the old man, Philipp Reiswig, could not be stopped. In November of 1883 he began the trip back to the land he had left. He acted solely on his own. He did not ask for any financial help from the church or the conference, and he did not receive any. He had planned to go to the Crimea, but when he reached Odessa his money gave out. And in order to buy a ticket for the rest of the trip, he sold his good high boots and used an old pair instead.

At this time Adventists could not publicly teach their doctrines in Russia. When L. R. Conradi tried to do missionary work there, the police put him in prison. They stopped other foreigners and sent them out of the country or halted their work by other methods.

But Reiswig invented his own successful method and continued his work more or less undisturbed for two years. Instead of allowing his handicaps to hinder him, he used them to his advantage. As he traveled from village to village, he carried tracts and papers. He went to the marketplace and singled out some likely person. Mentioning his poor eyesight, Reiswig would ask, "I have something interesting here. Would you be kind enough to read it to me?"

Few refused such a request. When the person had read a few sentences, Reiswig asked what he thought about it. Usually he received a favorable answer, perhaps out of sheer politeness or sympathy for an old man suffering from weak eyes. In this way he went from person to person, from home to home. Sometimes opposition rose up, but even the strongest opponents did not harm him. They realized if they attacked an old man such as he, it would only make their cause look weaker. So he continued on his way, and before long 30 people in the Crimea had begun to keep the Sabbath.

When Conradi told the story about his unlikely missionary he added this personal testimony: "Since that time, if a man wants to go out to work for the Lord, I have never hindered him. It is not by might or power, but by the Spirit of the Lord; and He can take old men, renew their strength, and in His strength, can do the work with them." [8]

Philipp Reiswig returned to America in 1886, but he did not stay long. The following year he went back to Russia with more literature. Now he added a new approach to his work. Having learned some hymns from his grandchildren he would go to a village marketplace and begin to sing. This, of course, attracted an audience, to which he then distributed his literature. After years of faithful witnessing, he went to his rest in Russia. At the funeral service the pastor said, "If everyone lived as this old man did, he surely would go to heaven."

Although Seventh-day Adventist work in Russia began small and seemed insignificant, the seed of the message had now been sown in a land that appeared closed to its proclamation. The following years proved that the seed was good, with potential for life and growth.

6 The First Church

L. R. Conradi (1856-1939), whose influence and work meant much to the early development of Adventism in Russia, was born in Karisruhe, Germany. He began studies leading to the Roman Catholic priesthood but later changed his mind and at the age of 17 emigrated to the United States. In the home of a Seventh-day Adventist farmer he found "present truth" through Bible studies and the family's personal influence. After his conversion he joined the remnant church through baptism. Ellen G. White noticed the talented young man and advised him to attend Battle Creek College. He went, meeting his college expenses by working as a typesetter at the Review and Herald Publishing Association. That he finished the four-year academic course in one year says something for his energy and talents.

In January 1886, the General Conference sent Conradi to Europe, where he led out in the German work. The newly organized General European Conference chose him as its first president in 1901. In 1903 he became a vice president of the General Conference. For a long time he served his church as Europe's leading administrator, evangelist, editor, and author.

An enormous capacity for work characterized Conradi. He revised and enlarged J. N. Andrews' *History of the Sabbath,* an important and time-consuming task. The fourth revised and enlarged edition of the book, published in 1912, lists both Andrews and Conradi as authors. He wrote a great number of books in German, several of which were translated into other languages. Numerous tracts, pamphlets, and articles poured from his prolific pen. Under his editorship the German *Herold der Wahrheit (Herald of Truth),* a biweekly publication, reached a circulation of 110,000. No other Adventist paper in Europe up to the present time has reached such a circulation. Gerhardt Rempel, current editor of *Advent Echo,* estimates that altogether from 12 to 15 million copies of books, tracts, and articles by Conradi reached his readers. The fact that he needed only three or four hours of sleep a night contributed to his productive ability.[1]

When this dynamic leader accepted Gerhard Perk's request to help the fledgling Sabbathkeepers in Russia, something was bound to happen, and it certainly did!

First Seventh-day Adventist Church Organized

On his way to Russia for his first visit in June 1886, Conradi met a converted Jew in Romania, a Presbyterian missionary in the employ of the English Bible Society. He informed Conradi that he probably would not be allowed to enter Russia as a minister of religion because of severe restrictions on representatives of religions other than the Russian Orthodox. The Jew knew this by his own experience. Therefore Conradi, in applying for a visa, took advantage of his former experience as a typesetter in Battle Creek and listed himself as a printer. The Russian consul in Romania signed his passport. On July 6 he crossed the border and traveled by train to Odessa, where he met Gerhard Perk, the Sabbathkeeping Bible colporteur. This man's knowledge of German and Russian made him invaluable as a translator. Without him Conradi's introductory experiences might have been even more frustrating.

Fortunately the details of what happened to the two men on their travels together are well documented. Gerhard Perk told the story to the General Conference session of 1909 and Conradi wrote about it at length, both in private letters and published material.

From Odessa the two traveled by steamer on the Black Sea to the Crimea, where they landed about 40 miles north of Sevastopol. Here they found several Sabbathkeepers, firstfruits of the elderly Philipp Resiwig's witnessing. After holding a series of meetings at a place called Japontschi, which enjoyed a steadily increasing attendance, Conradi decided to speak on the Sabbath question. This caused violent opposition. The next evening when he began to speak, enemies smashed the windows so forcefully that pieces of glass flew all over the room. Thus the troubles began.

Gerhard Perk says Conradi's activities alarmed the authorities, and they began searching for the man. The crisis climaxed in July at Berdebulat, where the believers planned a baptism. Nineteen convenanted to keep the commandments of God and the faith of Jesus, and they chose an elder and a deacon. The first Seventh-day Adventist church in Russia was now a reality. Two women united with the church through baptism. This solemn rite created quite a sensation among the people in a nearby Russian village. Some of them actually climbed on top of their houses to witness the baptism.

Such an event did not, of course, pass unnoticed by religious opponents and the authorities. Immediately following the baptism, the church members celebrated the ordinance of humility and were about to partake of the Lord's Supper when a representative from the sheriff's office entered and ordered Conradi to appear before the officer in a nearby house. Gerhard Perk went along to interpret.

The sheriff demanded their passports and then he wrote a statement accusing them of three crimes: (1) teaching Jewish heresy, (2) baptizing two women into the Jewish faith, and (3) proselytizing among Russians. He asked the men to sign this statement. They refused to do so for they did not consider themselves guilty of the charges. He also asked some Sabbathkeepers present to sign a statement that they would abstain from work on Sundays. They did not comply either, since it was not required by law. On Sundays buyers and sellers carried on a lively business at the local market. Nobody seemed worried about these Sundaykeepers who worked on that day!

Two of the new church members guaranteed that Conradi and Perk would appear the next day in the nearby town of Perekop to stand before the isprafnik, the highest officer in the district. Then the men returned to the Sabbath service and completed the Lord's Supper. The first Sabbath celebration of the first organized Seventh-day Adventist church in Russia had turned out to be exciting! But opponents of the infant church planned still more serious trouble.

In Perekop the next day, the isprafnik read a letter from the sheriff that, among other things, accused the two men of making Jews out of Christians. The official eyed them from head to foot and angrily shouted; ''We want no preachers in Russia!'' Two policemen took the pair outside the village to a large white building surrounded by a high wall. It turned out to be the ill-famed district prison.

Locked Up In Prison

The first sight that greeted Conradi and Perk as they entered the prison did nothing to encourage them. The jailer, trembling with rage, was striking a prisoner on each side of his face. Blood streamed from the prisoner's mouth but he just took off his shoe and used it as a spittoon so as not to soil the floor. They were revulsed as they witnessed this incident, but they could not help wondering if such treatment awaited them also. With longing eyes they looked through the barred windows at the open fields.

A little carelessness on the part of Perk nearly caused him to land in the prison's dungeon—the ''dark hole.'' He noticed graffiti written on the walls in the cell, most of it not exactly edifying. The guards had removed everything of value from the prisoners, but they overlooked a pencil in one of Perk's pockets. He decided to put something helpful on the walls, and wrote the first part of each of the Ten Commandments. When the isprafnik visited them, he noticed the writing and barked, "It is forbidden to write on the walls!" The jailer immediately decided to punish Perk by sending him down into the dungeon. The turnkey hastened him out, but as Perk paused to put on his boots the isprafnik intervened and ordered the turnkey to take him back into the cell. He felt fortunate to get off with only a severe scolding.

The food consisted mainly of heavy black rye bread and a soup at noon. The soup was not very appetizing but they were given plenty. The guards served it in a three- to four-gallon capacity wooden tub, and usually they needed only half of it. At one time a butcher brought a number of sheep heads and intestines to the prison for the benefit of the prisoners. Most of them welcomed the change in menu, but Perk says all he and Conradi received were the entrails!

During their 40-day imprisonment the uncertainty of their fate increased their misery. There were more than 80 prisoners in the jail, and the ones on their floor expected to be deported to Siberia. Several officials hinted that the Adventists would suffer the same fate. Even the jailer tried to frighten them. Through the hole in the door where he passed in their food, he noticed that the two men often knelt in prayer. " 'Your God will never hear you,' he taunted. 'You will go to Siberia!' " A day came, though, when the jailer confessed, "Your God did hear you." [2]

A judge said the men could be released on bail for 1,000 rubles—at that time the equivalent of $500. The believers immediately went to work gathering in their crops even though it was early, and selling them to raise the money. When they presented the amount, they learned to their great disappointment that only Perk could be released; Conradi had to remain in prison. Since Conradi did not speak any Russian the brethren decided to leave both men there, and the jailer returned the money. Later the believers found out that they had received a better price for the grain by selling it early than if they had waited until the usual time.[3]

American Connection Brings Relief

Upon his arrest, Conradi immediately tried to contact the American consul of Odessa by telegram and letter, as well as Adventist headquarters in Basel, Switzerland. On August 19 he received the following letter from the American consul at Odessa: "Your letter, dated August 4, 1886, was received at this consulate today. I will do all that is within my power to secure an early trial. I regret very much that you should have brought yourself in conflict with the Russian authorities on a question of religion. It is a subject on which they are very sensitive, and had I seen you, and known that the object of your journey was of a semireligious character, I would have warned you that the Russian authorities deal very severely with any effort of this nature. I have written to the governor of Simferopol, and also to the American minister at St. Petersburg, asking that immediate attention be given to your case. T. F. Heenan." [4]

A few days later he heard from the American minister in St. Petersburg, G.V.N. Lathrop. He promised to help, but pointed out the special laws of Russia that Conradi might have transgressed. He wrote: "I fear that it will be found that the laws of Russia forbid any minister of a foreign denomination of Christians, from coming into Russia and from teaching their distinctive views without special leave having been first granted. Therefore, I shall do all I can for your relief, but must say to you that the action of the foreign office is very slow." [5] Lathrop not only wrote to the minister of foreign affairs but went personally to the authorities and told them Conradi was not a Jew but a Christian.

It is difficult to understand from this distance in time how the two men dared to work publicly, proclaiming what the Orthodox Church considered heresy. The warning given by the American officials about Russian restrictions pointed out well-known facts. Czar Alexander III (1881-1894), married to Princess Dagmar of Denmark, ruled Russia at this time. He planned a complete Russification of the nation so that it would be one nationality, speak one language, and profess a single religion—the Orthodox. His advisers counseled him that the religious freedom granted by Catherine II when she invited oppressed religious people to settle in Russia was limited in time. They interpreted the "forever" of her decree to mean only 100 years. Since that period of time had passed they felt free to persecute the Jews and impose restrictions on all non-Orthodox religious groups.

It may be that Conradi trusted his American citizenship to keep him out of trouble as he and Perk openly tried to convert Russians, but his passport did not keep them from being arrested and spending nearly six weeks in a miserable prison. American influence was strong in Russia at that time, however, and it brought about comparatively fast results. High authorities gave the order for release. The minister of the interior sent the czar's order to the censor in Simferopol.

Finally on Friday, September 10, the prison gates opened, and Conradi and Perk breathed freely once more. They immediately hired a one-horse lumber wagon, the best available, and drove the 25 miles to Berdebulat, where the believers welcomed them wholeheartedly. The meeting that evening lasted far into the night! Conradi finally received good news from his family and the headquarters at Basel, and a package of *Reviews* and *Signs* delighted him.

Planting the Seed Firmly

One would think that after such an experience Conradi would hasten out of the country and back to his family and friends in the security of Switzerland. But he entertained no such thought! On Sabbath morning and evening he and Perk conducted long meetings, perfecting the church organization and establishing a tract society. The recent events seemed to increase interest, and several people expressed their desire to be baptized and unite with the church.

For nearly three more weeks Conradi and Perk, along with Oscar Roth, who had arrived from Basel, traveled extensively in eastern Russia. From Odessa they journeyed 1,500 miles to Saratov on the Volga River. Warned that opponents were trying to trump up an excuse for another arrest, they worked more carefully than before. They found many sympathizers and believers and encouraged and strengthened them in their faith.

Finally, after a visit of four months and 10 days, Conradi returned to Basel via Moscow, and Perk returned to his home. Tired but happy, Conradi knew of 80 persons in Russia who chose to obey the commandments of God and follow the faith of Jesus. His final word as he tells the story proved to be prophetic indeed: "The truth has found an entrance, the seed is firmly planted, and, God giving the increase, it will undoubtedly grow and prosper." [6]

7   Nothing Can Stop God's Purpose

Jacob Klein was born in a German settlement on the Volga River but emigrated to America. There he became an Adventist and began missionary work in Nebraska. Later, after a short training course in Hamburg, Germany, he went back to Russia as a missionary to the area where he had lived as a small child. When Klein arrived on the scene the local Orthodox priest thought Conrad Laubhan (1838-1923), an early Adventist worker who had visited the area before him, had returned. The police arrested Klein and put him in jail. The charge: "proselytizing Russians."

Because the czarist government's regulations against that kind of religious activity were strict, the charge was a serious one. A contemporary writer described two sections of the Russian Penal Code as it stood at that time:

"Section 187 declares that if any person tempts or persuades an adherent of the Russo-Greek Church to leave that church and join some other Christian denomination, he shall be banished to Siberia for life. Section 188 provides that if any person shall leave the Orthodox Church and join another Christian denomination, he shall be handed over to the ecclesiastical authorities for instruction and admonition; his minor children shall be taken into the custody of the government, his real estate shall be put into the hands of an administrator, and until he abjures his errors he shall have no further control over either." [1]

Klein did not speak Russian and defended himself by referring to that fact. The police did not believe him and imprisoned him, refusing him all food until he should confess he knew Russian. They released him after 17 days, but by that time hunger had weakened him so much that he stayed in bed for several weeks. His case dragged on for two years during which time the authorities retained his passport. As soon as the court acquitted him, he continued his soul-winning work.[2]

The brethren learned how to avoid getting into trouble as they worked among the German colonists. They would arrive in a town in the evening, arrange and hold a meeting immediately, then hasten on to the next place before word of their presence reached the local authorities and the priest. By the time the latter went into action, the workers were gone from the district.

The *Subbotniki*

It is easy for a Russian to understand which day of the week is the Bible Sabbath, since the Russian word for Saturday *(Subbota)* means Sabbath. At the time Seventh-day Adventists entered Russia, the standard Orthodox catechism used in teaching every school-child pointed out the relationship between Creation and the seventh-day Sabbath. It stated that while the Sabbath "is not entirely kept as a festival, still in memory of the creation of the world and in continuation of its original observance, it is distinguished from the other days of the week by a relaxation of the rule of fasting." [3]

Perhaps this explains one of the reasons the Adventist message found such a positive response in Russia in spite of the enormous obstacles for ministers and the unrelenting persecution of those who accepted it. By 1893 Conradi wrote that Adventists had more adherents in Russia than anywhere else in Europe. Although scores of members left for the United States, Argentina, and Brazil, taking with them the precious truth they had discovered, 500 stayed behind in Russia to let their light shine there.[4] The work had begun several years earlier in

Western Europe, but no country there had achieved such results. It is also interesting to note that even in 1986 the 31,000 Adventists in the atheist Soviet Union who openly confess their faith number more than the members in any other European country except Romania.

The 500 Seventh-day Adventists in Russia in 1893 were not the only Sabbathkeepers in the country. As early as 1875 John N. Andrews noted, in his first report to the General Conference from Europe, "There are, I think, from all that I can learn, many thousand Sabbathkeepers in Russia. I am extremely anxious to open communication with them and to establish a permanent minister there. Can you not find a Russian Sabbathkeeper in the United States?"[5]

Perhaps the "many thousand Sabbathkeepers" he refers to belonged to some of the Judaizing groups known as far back as the fifteenth century, and the quasi-Jewish sect that developed at the end of the eighteenth century and survived into Soviet times. All members of this latter group were Gentiles; some historians divide them into capless *subbotniki* and cap-wearing ones. They discard the New Testament and accept only the Old. They do, however, refuse to work on Saturdays, and this similarity with Adventists caused some confusion. As this peculiar sect is fast dying out, the expression *subbotniki* refers now more and more to the growing Seventh-day Adventist Church.

Aside from these Jewish-influenced sectarians, there are indications that Bible-believing Christians, through studying the inspired Word of God, found the Sabbath truth long before Conradi and Park organized the first Seventh-day Adventist church in Berdebulat in the Crimea. One such Christian served as an officer in the czarist army. His dramatic experience and suffering for his faith and practice came to light in 1893. An Adventist minister heard of a well-educated Russian woman who kept the Sabbath and wrote her a letter asking how she found the light. Her answer tells the story of an early

AIR-5

Sabbathkeeping martyr in Russia.

He Remained Faithful Until Death

The unique testimony of this lonely Sabbathkeeper and the experiences her courageous father passed through can hardly leave any reader untouched. She began her story with these words, written in reply to the pastor:

"You wish to know, dear brother, how I came to observe the Sabbath. The question I can scarcely answer with few words; I must rather give you a short biography of my father." [6] She goes on to tell how her father, a member of the state church and an officer in the Russian Army, found the Sabbath truth through studying the Bible. He required his children to follow the Bible strictly from early childhood. He told them to study the Bible secretly and warned them they might suffer persecution because of their faith.

Less than a year after her marriage to a Finn, the authorities banished her father to a monastery on a northern island because of his faith. They sent some of his children to monasteries and later exiled them to the Caucasus and Siberia. Although she and her husband escaped imprisonment and exile, the police kept close track of them.

Her letter to the pastor continues: "Fifteen years passed, and during this time I heard scarcely anything of my father. Finally my sister, who is now dead, and I decided to hunt our father in Siberia. But what did we see? Horrible! The impression of what I there saw and heard had such an effect upon me that ever since my hair has turned gray. But we had to rise above our despair, the thought that we do not know the ways of God giving us consolation; for it is written that He is wonderful in counsel and excellent in working. Through the intervention of an Englishman my father was finally transferred to another monastery, but when we found him there, he fared even worse. He had consumed away, seemed very weak, and had only one eye left. I fainted when I saw him." [7]

The daughter pleaded with General Paschkoff to intercede for her father. This led to a short reprieve. Immediately her father began to publish a missionary journal and kept it going for five years. But when he was 82 years old the police arrested him and put him in prison. Although the same general interceded for him, the authorities decided to place him in an insane asylum, but death intervened.

In describing her father's death, his daughter went on to say: "Even during his last moments his greatest burden was to impress us with the commandments of Jehovah and the faith of Jesus, and to point us to the glorious appearing of our Lord and Saviour Jesus Christ." [8]

The letter tells how this faithful officer's daughter prayed for years that she would find someone who also believed in the Sabbath truth. All other groups she contacted did not observe the seventh day. One can imagine her joy to receive this letter from a Seventh-day Adventist pastor and to learn that thousands observed the Sabbath and looked forward to Christ's coming. She brought her letter to a close, saying that she constantly prayed to her heavenly Father "to make me worthy to be the daughter of my father, who was suffered 30 long years for the sake of God's holy truth." [9]

This officer's experience confirms what is stated in other sources, that for centuries Russian monasteries maintained prisons for "heretics," where thousands of honest inquirers languished or met a painful death. The Protestant Reformation enlightened a great part of Europe, but Russia remained in the grip of the medieval Russian Orthodox Church, which, backed by the czarist regime, used harsh measures to strike down dissenters.

When Conradi passed through Moscow in 1886 after his prison experience in the Crimea, he saw a sight that showed the power of the state church and the respect the priests received from the people. He wrote:

"On my way I noticed a fine carriage with six large black

horses driving through the streets. As it passed, everyone uncovered his head, bowed reverently, and crossed himself. It stopped beside a chapel, and the people, rich and poor, rushed up to it, some gentlemen and ladies even leaving their carriages. Drawing nearer, I saw in it two priests clad in rich garments, one holding a light and a large cross. The people kissed the cross, and the hands of the priests, and even the seams of their garments.'' [10]

It is understandable that any teaching that might weaken such power over the people would be strongly resisted by the state church.

Other Protestant leaders also suffered. At a time when the czar visited Copenhagen, Denmark, leading members of the Evangelical Alliance from several European countries and America delivered a petition on behalf of Lutheran pastors in the Baltic provinces. In his answer on behalf of the emperor, the procurator of the Holy Synod referred to the previous attitude of the Roman Catholic Church in Poland and the old Teutonic knights in the Baltic provinces and tried to prove that their descendants still showed the same intolerant spirit. He then said:

''In Russia, the Western churches, far from having freed themselves from their domineering pretensions, are always ready to attack not only the power, but also the unity of our country. Russia cannot grant them the liberty to proselytize; it will never permit its children to be taken from the Orthodox Church, to be enrolled in the ranks of strange confessions, which have themselves not even laid down the ancient arms once raised against her. Russia declares it openly in its laws, and leaves it with the highest justice of Him who alone directs the destinies of empires.'' [11]

Stomping on Fire Spreads It

The persecution sometimes caused the opposite effect from what the persecutors intended. The experience of the apostolic church clearly repeated itself in Russia. The enemies of the emerging Christian church tried to stop its growth, but their efforts only advanced the work further, as stomping on fire oftentimes spreads the flame. The religious leaders "called the apostles in, had them whipped, and after ordering them never to speak in the name of Jesus, set them free. As the apostles left the Council, they were happy, because God had considered them worthy to suffer disgrace for the sake of Jesus. And every day in the Temple and in people's homes they continued to teach and preach the Good News about Jesus the Messiah" (Acts 5:40-42, TEV).

The opposition, threats, and physical torture only encouraged the apostles to work more intensely than before. Something else of great importance also happened as a result of these first difficult days. The Pharisee "Saul tried to destroy the church; going from house to house, he dragged out the believers, both men and women, and threw them into jail" (Acts 8:3). As some of them managed to flee out of the country, note what took place: "That very day the church in Jerusalem began to suffer cruel persecution. All the believers, except the apostles, were scattered through the provinces of Judea and Samaria. . . . The believers who were scattered went everywhere, preaching the message (verses 1-4, TEV).

At the end of the nineteenth century the experience of the Russian believers again proved that violence cannot permanently hinder God's purposes. In about 1891, in the middle of winter, the authorities seized all the men in one flourishing Seventh-day Adventist church, chained them together, and forced them to walk 500 miles across the Caucasus Mountains near Gerusi, close to the border of Persia (now Iran).

With only women and children left, the persecutors thought the church would die. But they were mistaken. The women said, "God lives. If we ever worked, we will work now. The worst they can do is to send us where our husbands and fathers have gone." [12] In a short time church membership doubled!

The men shared their faith also. They spent a year in an exile colony, where they faithfully sowed the seed of truth. Later, when the situation improved, the church sent a colporteur to work where the men had witnessed. He sent back a telegram: "Over a hundred keeping the Sabbath. Eighty ready for baptism. Send a minister." [13]

In 1927 the Siberian Seventh-day Adventist Conference held its session in the city of Omsk in western Siberia. Delegates and visitors met in the Lutheran Catherine Church. The reports referred to churches established in places so remote that no roads led to them. Workers could reach them only by riding on horseback. How did they come into existence? Persons fleeing from religious persecution during the time of the czars or persons fearing the new oppression of the revolution founded some of the churches. They sought refuge in the Altai Mountains, and spread the light. That year 300 new members joined the 107 churches; this brought the Siberian membership to 2,342. [14]

Referring to how persecution brought Seventh-day Adventists to Siberia, both as exiles and as refugees, Walter Kolarz fittingly remarks: "This is how Seventh-day Adventism came to Siberia. The czarist government unwittingly met the traveling expense of the Adventist missionaries." [15]

Joseph Wolff Prepared the Way

Joseph Wolff (1795-1862), called "the missionary to the world" by Ellen G. White, was part of the Great Awakening movement in the mid-nineteenth century. He visited Russia, proclaiming the imminence of Christ's second coming and fixing the date a few years prior to William Miller's 1844. Wolff's teachings affected several members of a religious movement called Molokans, who believed Christ would return in 1833. Their name means "milk drinkers." They preferred to be known as "Spiritual Christians," but accepted the name because instead of fasting during Lent, they drank milk. "We already drink the milk of paradise!'' they explained.

Religious persecution caused the Molokans to flee from central Russia to the Caucasus. In 1895 two Adventist families exiled to the same area studied the Bible with them. Tracts printed on very thin paper so that they could easily be enclosed in letters also reached this place. Soon 150 Molokans in an isolated mountain colony became Sabbathkeepers. When H. J. Loebsack, the first ordained Russian minister, visited them the first time he received a unique welcome:

"About 50 men had gathered together to give us a reception upon the streets of this village. The women and children were clothed as for a festival and they stood upon the flat roofs of the houses to receive us. . . . When evening came they asked the privilege of taking off our shoes, and every mealtime we were invited to another family.'' [16]

On Sabbath morning Loebsack organized a church of 31 men and women. Later they arranged for the baptism of 46 new members. The weather was so cold the candidates had to push ice aside to get into the water, but no one wanted to wait to be baptized.

The Spirit of the Lord worked directly on the hearts of neighbors and friends who noticed the quiet witness given by the lives of the believers. A letter written in 1895 by a Russian member illustrates this point. While he and other Sabbathkeepers gathered for worship they saw a neighboring family go into the fields to harvest. In the middle of the group's Bible study the neighbor, followed by his wife and children, left their field. With two scythes over his shoulders he strode into the worship service, the rest of the family trailing behind. All wept.

Surprised, the Sabbathkeepers hardly knew what to say. When finally they asked why the family came, the neighbor said, ''When we began to harvest, a voice seemed to speak to me again and again saying, 'Today is the day of the Lord, a holy day.' And I could work no longer in the field.'' The writer of the letter closed by saying, ''Today they united with us.''

71

8

Faithful Believers Help the Church to Grow

With their membership increasing steadily, the churches in southern Russia organized into a conference in 1909. Its first president, Daniel Isaac, reported four workers, 16 churches, and 572 members. These figures may not seem impressive today, but considering the lack of religious freedom and what new believers faced when they left the Orthodox Church, the growth was remarkable.

One of the four ministers in the newborn conference, a Russian, held a series of meetings in the city of Sevastopol. As a result, 62 persons, among them sailor-soldiers, joined the church. The police immediately arrested three of the sailors and deported to the city of Arkhangelsk in the Far North. Situated at the mouth of the Dvina River close to the White Sea, the city is icebound six months of the year. (Founded in the 1580s, it takes its name from the famous fortified monastery of the Archangel Michael, which still exists.)

The three sailors came under heavy pressure because of their religious beliefs. Persecutors required them to work on the Sabbath and attend services in the state church. When they refused to break the Sabbath or to pray to images, they were flogged. They appealed to the authorities in these words: "Let us keep the Sabbath, and do not force us to worship the things which man has made. You may punish us otherwise all you please." [1]

A priest was called from St. Petersburg to persuade them to

return to their former faith. When they refused his efforts they were bound with fetters and even had to pay the travel expenses for the priest! During the time they spent in a naval prison one of them wrote to a minister: "I still have $10. Please pay $2 of this as tithe into the treasury of the Lord, 70 cents as six months' donation for Sabbath school, 70 cents as an annual offering, and 60 cents to the poor sister. Also take from this money enough to pay for your postage on the letter that you write to me. We are at Kronstadt near St. Petersburg, in the navy prison, where we expect to receive our fourth court sentence, which may be to work in a chain gang. But we are determined not to forsake the truth." [2]

All over Russia the growth continued, faster than anywhere else in Europe. During nine months of 1904 more than 500 new members joined the Adventists; by the end of that year the total membership was 1,920. [3]

Political Upheavals Bring Changes

The tumultuous years of Russia's catastrophic war with Japan, and the internal revolution and political upheavals that followed from 1905 to 1907, brought about some changes for religious minorities. A parliamentary body called the Duma was elected. It functioned only 10 weeks, followed by the second Duma eight months later. They demanded reforms, such as greater religious freedom and equal rights for Jews and other religious dissenters, from the czarist regime. Although the rulers never fully met these demands, they did introduce some improvements, at least temporarily.

In December of 1905 a comparatively large general meeting of Seventh-day Adventists convened right in the capital city of St. Petersburg. More than 100 persons representing Russians, Germans, Estonians, and Lettonians took part. The following year, conference and mission leaders signed and sent a memorial to Czar Nicolas II. In it they declared their loyalty to the emperor. At the same time other religious minorities demonstrated their loyalty to the rulers. Evidently the Adventist memorial pleased the czar, for he wrote across it: "I thank these good people for their kind wishes and their prayers. Nicolas." [4] On November 6 of the same year the minister of the interior issued an imperial edict granting Seventh-day Adventists liberty to propagate their doctrines freely, notifying civil government "to avoid all uncertainties in the religious affairs of the Adventists." [5] A new day seemed about to dawn. The situation eased somewhat, but in actual practice officials continued to restrict religious activities.

The following year the Adventists organized their first union conference, approximately 2,500 members in three conferences and three missions. Until then the field had formed part of the German Union. The new organizations began to function on January 1, 1908. J. T. Boettcher became the union's first president. In geographical area, this constituted the largest union ever organized in the Adventist Church, either before that time or since. It stretched from the shores of the Baltic Sea to the Pacific Ocean, and from the Arctic Ocean in the north to the Black Sea in the south. It embraced one sixth of the earth's total landmass.

Literature for Russia was published in Hamburg, Germany. Previously literature for Russia had been printed in Basel, Switzerland, but censors subjected any literature printed in Switzerland to careful scrutiny and possible refusal, because many Russian revolutionaries sought refuge there. And a high duty was levied on literature imported into Russia. In 1908 Adventists obtained permission to establish a branch of the German publishing house near union headquarters in Riga. Although the authorities soon found an excuse for closing the branch in Riga, the church managed to find a private but government-authorized company that did the printing for them at a favorable rate.

The Russian censor sanctioned Ellen G. White's *Christian Temperance* for printing. This was a great boon to the colporteurs, who for the first time could sell a legally approved book. Records do not indicate in what language the book was printed.

About the same time a Dr. V. Pampaian began medical work in Armenia, in the area of Mount Ararat. A group of believers lived near the little town of Nachitschewan, which means "we have rested here for the first time." According to local tradition, Noah built this city; a churchyard supposedly contains Noah's tomb. Fanatical tribespeople created some problems for Dr. Pampaian. One evening they broke into his home and stole or broke to pieces his surgical instruments. He himself fled and took refuge with the Russian policemen. But he continued working as a medical missionary.

Primarily a Missionary Movement

After the 1905 revolution the czar introduced martial law and maintained it for several years. Often the authorities used this as an excuse to place limits on the religious freedom promised in the edict issued by the ministry of the interior. Adventists, therefore, continued to take precautions in some of their activities in order not to provoke trouble. Baptisms, for instance, often were conducted at midnight or very early in the morning.

At one place the local church ended its regular evening meeting about 10:30 p.m., and the congregation began to walk quietly out of the town to conduct a midnight baptism. But a double surprise awaited them. As they reached the edge of town they found a crowd waiting to accompany them. By the time they arrived at the baptismal site, the crowd had swelled to about 150 and included three policemen, the town physician, and a soldier. Some in the crowd were drunk and evidently had not come for any good purpose. The church members feared what might happen.

As they began the service they had their second surprise. The policemen whom they feared turned out to be their friends.

One even volunteered to ask the people to remove their hats during the service. But the pastor said he would leave that to each person to decide. When they began singing the first hymn, however, everyone uncovered his head, and the people maintained quiet and order throughout the service.

In 1911 the leaders divided the territory of the union. Local conferences in the far eastern portion were organized into the Siberian Union, with 826 members. By the end of that year this figure had increased to 1,007. The long winters and intense cold made travel an ordeal. In visiting the churches, ministers had to travel as many as 1,000 miles at a time, most of it by sleigh pulled by dogs or horses. Temperatures of -69° F (-56° C) pierced through their double suits and heavy eight pound felt boots. The first effect of such severe cold is deceptive, since it feels similar to heat. Travelers sometimes had to call one another's attention to frozen noses and ears, but rubbing the affected part with snow soon started the blood circulating again. Sometimes hungry wolves attacked them. Yet, one of the pastors wrote that they worked hardest in winter, because then the rivers and swamps were frozen and travel at that time afforded ''greater comfort and convenience''!

On a visit to Russia in 1912 L. R. Conradi attended the Siberian Union committee meeting. During the meetings three ministers were ordained and assigned to different missions in the huge Siberian field. In a letter written July 7 to A. G. Daniells and W. A. Spicer, Conradi commented: ''When we considered that some of these missions are as large as the United States in territory, we can realize what a relief it is to the superintendent of such a field when he has at least one additional ordained minister in his mission.''

The new organizations did not function well in some places because the executive committees did not get permission to meet. In addition, police closed some churches, drove the people out, and ministers were prosecuted and sentenced. The church leaders believed this was not in harmony with the czar's wishes, so in 1912 they appointed a deputation to meet the minister of the interior in St. Petersburg. They talked with his representative, Mr. Kalatarov. A deputation also met with the director of the Department for Religious Affairs of Foreign Sects. He told them that the Russian government did not recognize a union or a conference, only a local church. He also said that ministers could not legally travel from place to place visiting churches and giving lectures. Things certainly looked discouraging to the members, but believing in their special mission, they carried on.

Opposition Creates Opportunities

Opposition in written form also appeared early in the history of Adventism in Russia. Ten years after Conradi organized the first church, he mentioned a book widely circulated at the annual fair at Nizhny Novgorod, the largest and most famous fair in Russia. It attracted traders from all over the country as well as from Europe and Asia. The book contained statistical data and doctrinal information about the new sects in the country. A good share of the content dealt with Adventism. Among other things, it presented the church's view on the Sabbath, the immortality question, and the second advent of Christ. The author quoted Bible texts that ministers used to support their doctrines. Because of this, the book appealed positively to its readers instead of warning them away. Believers suggested to Conradi that the church should buy a good supply of the books and circulate them!

In 1911 an even more important book came off the official presses. S. D. Bondar, of the Ministry of the Interior in St. Petersburg, a learned man who spoke eight languages, was assigned to write a book about Seventh-day Adventists. He prepared well for his task. Not only did he visit several conferences and meetings, listen to the speakers, and interview the leaders, but he also bought all the larger Adventist books available in German and English. He studied *History of the*

Sabbath, by J. N. Andrews and L. R. Conradi, and the 1910 and 1911 *SDA Yearbooks*. He interviewed J. T. Boettcher, president of the Russian Union. Evidently Boettcher looked upon the result with pleasure, for when the book came out he exclaimed, "It is the best thing I ever saw in print!" [6]

The author explained all the main doctrines of the church, referred to Uriah Smith's interpretation of the prophecies in Daniel and Revelation, and explained the organizational structure from the local church to the General Conference. Once again a book printed by the government and reviewed by the newspapers, instead of hindering the Adventists as intended, promoted them. "We praise the Lord that He even now uses the government to help forward this cause," [7] commented Boettcher.

Concerning the missionary spirit of the church, the book made this striking statement: "The Seventh-day Adventists in Russia show a splendid, live, and active work. The movement continues to take in new districts in the European and Asiatic Russias. They reveal a determinate zeal in their missionary efforts to win souls. The whole organization is primarily a missionary one. . . . Every church member must help forward the third angel's message, and be a witness for Christ." [8] No wonder the opponents of the Adventist Church faced problems when they tried to quench it!

Even the priests of the Orthodox Church could not avoid hearing the witness of the Adventists. At a congress of the state church held in Kiev in 1909, the 1,000 priests present passed a resolution condemning Adventists. Boettcher saw in this a unique opportunity to witness for his faith. He asked the congress secretary for permission to inform the priests about what the Adventist Church really believed and practiced. His request granted, he took an hour and a half to explain the fundamentals of the Adventist faith to a packed and attentive audience.

Financially, the work in Russia reached a self-supporting

status by 1911. It even operated and paid for a Russian department at Friedensau Missionary School in Germany. Before World War I broke out in 1914, the membership in Russia had increased to 5,880 members, who were organized into 240 churches and employed 40 ministers.[9]

9

When the Course of History Was Changed

At about 9:00 p.m. on October 25, 1917, from its anchorage on the Neva River in the city of Petrograd, the Russian crusier *Aurora* fired blank shots. Those shots brought far-reaching and long-lasting consequences. The provisional government that had taken over on March 16, 1917, after Czar Nicholas II's abdication collapsed. Nine months later he and his family fell before a firing squad, ending any chance for the 300 year rule of the Romanov dynasty to be revived. Not just the Russian Empire but the entire world shook. Some say it still shakes!

The shots signaled an attack on the czar's winter palace, where most government officials were staying. The red flag of Bolshevism flew from the *Aurora's* mast, and revolutionaries occupied the Peter and Paul Fortress across the Neva. Since powerful guns of the fort were aimed directly at the Winter Palace, the government officials were forced to surrender. V. L. Lenin, founder of Bolshevism and mastermind of the revolution, succeeded in his coup. The course of world history was changed.

The indescribable sufferings the people went through during the following five years of civil war, foreign intervention, and famine touched many Adventist families. Some people, especially children, died from the starvation, typhus, cholera, and dysentery that ravaged the country. In 1921 Daniel Isaac, president of the East Russian Union, managed to attend a

AIR-6

European Division meeting at Skodsborg Sanitarium in Denmark. His firsthand report of the situation and the information he gave about the possibilities for transport led to a shipment of food from Sweden to Moscow. The Russian government approved the establishment of an Adventist relief organization under the direction of I. A. Lvov.[1] The following year, L. H. Christian went to Russia, sponsored by an international relief body led by the Norwegian philanthropist, Dr. Fritjof Nansen. Christian found the authorities cooperative. They transported all foodstuffs free of charge and guaranteed delivery without loss from theft, confiscation, or other causes. Church leaders in Moscow sent 600 tons of rye and several thousand food packages to Adventist pastors and elders in different cities. In cooperation with local officials, they distributed the supplies to the needy. The church established food kitchens that fed hundreds of children, each receiving one pound of bread and a bowl of soup per day.

The increased criminal activity under civil war conditions led to the murder of some Adventists; however, no reports exist of church members losing their lives in military action. Evidently the fact that the church did its utmost to stay out of politics played a role in saving some lives. Nevertheless, the radical change of government affected the church in many ways.

The Golden Decade

People in Western countries generally assume that government suppression of non-Orthodox churches continued when the Communists took control. That view hardly harmonizes with the facts. During the first years following the revolution, the evangelical churches enjoyed a degree of religious freedom they had never experienced under the empire.

One of the first decrees Lenin signed separated the church from the state. This introduced a new day for the religious groups that had suffered discrimination because of the intimate state-church partnership. Some writers call the following years the "golden decade" for evangelicals. The intense activity of the churches under the new conditions of liberty led to such a growth that the major Communist paper, *Pravda,* complained: "The clergy and sectarians developed a frenzied propaganda, and we deceive ourselves if we assert that only old men and women go to church." [2]

The minority churches accepted the "separation decree" of January 23, 1928, with special joy. The government published it under the title "Freedom of Conscience and of Religious Societies." The first three articles state:

1. "The church is separated from the state."

2. "Within the confines of the republic it is prohibited to issue any local laws or regulations restricting limiting freedom of conscience, or establishing privileges or preferential rights of any kind based upon the religious confession of the citizens."

3. "Every citizen may profess any religion or none. All restrictions of rights connected with the profession of any belief whatsoever, or with the nonprofession of any belief are annulled." [3]

The many people imprisoned or exiled to faraway places because of their religious activities welcomed the decree. Prison doors opened, and deported persons returned to their loved ones. The churches received them with great joy, some even meeting returning exiles outside city limits with songs and instrumental music.

In a written report H. J. Loebsack named the following 11 ministers who returned from exile in Siberia or other remote regions: A. Clement, S. Jefimow, J. Gorelik, J. G. Jacques, J. Sproghe, J. Gardischar, G. A. Grigoriev, M. Grietz, G. Gobel, A. Gontar, and Pastor Manschura. A twelfth, A. Osol, died during his exile. All had remained faithful through their severe trials, and they returned to their posts as church leaders. One of them, G. A. Grigoriev, led the church in Russia from 1934 to 1952.

When the "separation decree" first opened prison doors, the church received some new information. The Ministry of Religion told them that 70 young men who had refused to take up arms because of their religious convictions had been sentenced to hard labor in chains. Their terms ranged from 2 to 16 years. New government regulations opened the way for alternative service within the military.

Growth While the Law Permitted Religious Propaganda

Like all other religious minorities, Adventists took the "separation decree" at face value as a Magna Carta for a new day. This attitude was strengthened when the constituent assembly of the October Revolution adopted the Constitution of the Russian Soviet Republic in July of 1918. Article 13 stated: "The liberty of religious as well as antireligious propaganda is granted to all citizens." To make things even clearer and to avoid misunderstandings, the People's Commissariat of Justice issued an *Instruction* one month later on August 24. It specified that the January decree applied to all religious communions or confessions: "The Orthodox, the Old Ritualists, the Catholic of all rites, the Armenian-Gregorian, the Protestant, as well as Mohammedan, Buddhist, and Lamaic confessions."

These statements certainly harmonized with the writings of V. I. Lenin a few years earlier. Mentioning the "disgraceful laws" against people who did not hold the Orthodox creed, such as schismatics, sectarians, and Jews, he wrote: "These laws either forbid the existence of such faith or forbid its propagation. . . . All these laws are most unjust and oppressive. They are imposed by force alone. Everyone should have the right not only to believe what he likes but also to propagate whatever faith he likes."

This article 13, which permitted religious propaganda, is not valid today, because of changes in the constitution. The present wording states: "Citizens of the U.S.S.R. are guaranteed freedom of conscience, that is, the right to profess or not to profess any religion, and to conduct religious worship or atheistic propaganda.'' According to this, atheists kept the right to conduct propaganda, while religious people lost it. They retained only the right to ''worship.'' [4] But as long as article 13 of the July 1918 constitution remained valid and respected, it meant much to the religious bodies.

Six years after the revolution, H. J. Loebsack referred to an appeal issued by the Ministry of the Interior in its official paper. It stated that all adherents of any religious group need not remain in hiding any longer. If they lived abroad, the government offered them grants of land if they would return.

Loebsack describes conditions at that time: ''All our evangelistic efforts we carry on unmolested in the villages and cities, in our homes, and places of worship. All our workers enjoy permission to continue their work, with the exception of one who has meanwhile also been set free.'' This brought quite a change from the situation 14 years earlier as described by an Adventist leader: ''I have seen long-bearded men standing before the doors of our meeting houses in the large cities on the Volga, imploring us, with tears in their eyes, to let them come in and hear the message, the very one they had been waiting for, as they claimed; but a priest and a policeman would sit in the door and prevent everybody [who was not a member] from coming in.''

The Adventist leader also pointed out an interesting statistical fact as he wrote about membership growth. He mentioned that Adventists took a full 20 years to win 2,045 people for the message. But during the first nine months of 1923 they added 2,112. In other words, in less than a year they won more people than in the previous 20 years! Joyfully he wrote, ''From Mount Ararat to the Polar Sea, from the river Amur in the far east to the borders of Poland in the west, the Lord has impressed His seal upon the work of the third angel's message. We are grateful to the Lord for His stately steppings in our midst.''

85

As the message spread throughout this vast country it was accepted by many of the various nationalities that live there. In 1929 there were members of the following nationalities:

Armenians	Grusiners	Russians
Assyrians	Gypsies	Russiners
Bulgarians	Jews	Syrians
Buradens	Karaimens	Tartars
Czechs	Latvians	Tscheremissens
Estonians	Lithuanians	Tschuwaschens
Finns	Magyars	Ukrainians
Germans	Moldavians	White Russians
Góraliers	Mordvinens	Wodjakens
Greeks	Poles	

Freedom to Worship

Soon after the revolution the authorities turned two of the Adventist meeting places in Moscow into dwellings because of the need for housing. But an Armenian church, the first one built in Russia, opened its doors to them. The Armenians used their church only a few times a year on special feast days, so sharing the church building was not inconvenient to either of the congregations. The church seated about 200 people, and on several occasions it proved too small. When, for instance, Loebsack arranged for the wedding of one of his daughters in the church, the limited seating capacity forced many guests to stand outside during the ceremony. This Armenian church building still stands in the central part of Moscow, but it needs restoration. A famous painting on its ceiling represents the throne of God as described by the prophet Ezekiel.

The new conditions of comparative freedom were used to great advantage when the Adventists held their Fifth All-Russian Congress in Moscow August 1924. Delegates from all over the country, from the farthest borders of eastern Siberia to central Asia and from the shores of the Baltic and Arctic seas, attended. The Adventists rented a former Orthodox seminary for the session and used it both for meetings and sleeping quarters. They noted with special interest that the year of the seminary's founding coincided with the year so important to Adventism, 1844. This date, inscribed over the entrance, greeted them every time they entered the building. The newspapers carried advertisements for the evening meetings, inviting the general public to attend. As a climax to the meetings, the church arranged for a public baptism of 53 persons in one of Moscow's suburban parks. Just a few years previous, no one imagined that such events could take place in the capital city.

About this same time Adventists in Leningrad held their services in two large Lutheran churches called St. Michael's and St. Mary's, situated in prominent sections of the city. The members did not have enough money to buy heating fuel for the buildings during the cold winter months but they attended anyway, even when the temperature dropped below freezing. If the sun was shining, they went *outside* between the Sabbath school and church services to warm up a little!

It surprises many to learn that the first time Seventh-day Adventists sponsored the printing of Bibles it happened in the Soviet Union. The church took the initiative in this case because of the need. One report says that in Siberia a single copy of the Bible sold for the equivalent of $100, and in other parts of the country people exchanged a cow or a horse for a Bible. In cooperation with the Evangelical Society, which took care of the technical arrangements, a large-print edition came off the presses in Leningrad in 1926. A pocket edition printed in Kiev followed. The smaller edition was reproduced phototypographically from the larger one.

Adventists received 10,000 copies of the Bible from the two editions. In flexible leather binding, the Leningrad edition sold for eight rubles; in linen, three and a half rubles. When W. A. Spicer, then president of the world Seventh-day Adventist Church, received a copy bound in leather with gilt edges, he wrote, "This is a work of art, a credit to printers and binders. Really it is as beautiful a piece of bookmaking as I have seen."

Another event about this time delighted Adventists: the printing of 5,000 copies of a Russian Adventist hymnal with music. During the preceding 40 years of its existence, the church used hymnals purchased from the Baptists. Now they enjoyed their own hymnal, which contained 525 hymns, mostly of Russian origin. Although the situation for religion remained problematic, compared to the hardships suffered by non-Orthodox groups before the revolution these first years of the new regime appeared to the believers to be a "golden decade."

10 Adventists in Christian Communes

Stalin's forced collectivization of private farms in the late twenties fills many pages in history books. Less well known is the strange fact that Christian communal farms functioned in Communist Russia. Various religious groups, including Seventh-day Adventists, founded such communities.

In 1985 I met an Adventist man in Moscow who remembered his boyhood days in the little village of Smirnovka, near Rostov-on-Don, where such a commune existed. Almost everyone in the village belonged to the Seventh-day Adventist church, and about 200 banded together to form a commune. They shared everything except the most private things in common. His story made me curious to find out more about such projects, which appear as one of the greatest anomalies ever to surface in a Communist country, and certainly contrary to other events taking place in Russia. The Communist system, under its atheistic government, aims at gathering all business under state ownership and operation. The entire country today demonstrates this. How could Christian communal farms operate under such circumstances?

During the famine in the early twenties, government officials discovered that Protestants produced the best crops. An influential Communist, Bonch-Bruevich, who served as Lenin's secretary, undertook a scholarly study of a possible sectarian role in the proletarian revolution. Although he completely rejected their religious views, he admired their economical efficiency. He even published an article in the leading newspaper, *Pravda,* in which he described the sectarians as "exemplary toilers" who formed an economic vanguard in the countryside. He considered it not merely wrong but actually criminal not to use them for Russia's economic development.[1]

Bonch-Bruevich presented his view to leading Communist statesman Mikhail I. Kalinin, the formal head of the Soviet state from 1919 to 1946. Kalinin, a peasant by birth, ranked as the farming expert in the supreme Soviet leadership. He agreed with Bonch-Bruevich and decided to press for an official action promoting cooperation with the millions of sectarians.

At the Thirteenth Communist Party Congress in May 1924 Kalinin initiated the much-discussed point 17 of the congress resolution: "A specially attentive attitude must be shown to the sectarians, of whom many were cruelly persecuted by the Czarist regime and among whom there is now much activity. Through a skillful approach we must achieve that the considerable economic and cultural potentialities of the sectarians are directed into the channels of Soviet work. As the sectarians are numerous, this endeavor has great importance." [2]

In spite of strong opposition, the congress voted Kalinin's proposal. The Commissariat of Agriculture, which understood better than anyone else the large role religious farms played in the economy, showed firm support. Some even suggested that the state hand over all its decaying farms to them. Experience provided a good basis for such opinions, because four years earlier the authorities had begun transferring farm lands to the sectarians, and the results spoke favorably of their efficiency.

Adventist Communal Farms

One of the early Adventist communes was named Bratskii Trug ("Brotherly Labor") and operated near Krasgorod in the Ukraine.[3] In 1922 an able peasant and good organizer named

Konrad Kalinichenka requested permission to establish a small "Zion" for Adventist believers who desired to move into the greater Zion at Christ's coming. The Communist rulers cared nothing for doctrines regarding the Second Coming, but hunger plagued the population and they looked with favor on any project that promised increased food production.

The authorities evidently trusted Kalinichenka; he wisely kept his distance from religious fanatics of the time who went to extremes in communal life. They placed 500 acres of good farmland from a former estate at his disposal. About 200 Adventists of the area immediately began working together. They built dormitories, schools, a place of worship, a kitchen, a laundry, a tailor shop, and a shoe shop. Then they moved into the dormitories and lived together like one big family. They shared everything except spouses, children, and clothing.

The commune soon proved not only its farming ability but also its capacity to organize and produce. It never needed financial support from the government. It actually donated money to local cultural projects and supported the poor in the surrounding settlements. No wonder it earned high respect.

The commune's leaders assigned knowledgeable and experienced persons to each branch of the operation. They followed an effective four-part crop rotation system, cattle breeding, wheat production, and fruit and vegetable gardens. Soon the farm owned hundreds of excellent breeding cattle, dozens of good horses, hundreds of sheep, a multitude of different fowl, and 300 beehives in special apiaries. The members built huge barns for the grain, and skilled people operated steam mills and dairy plants.

A seven-member council, consisting of leaders from the different operations and directed by Konrad Kalinichenka, managed the commune. If any major problem arose, the council called a general meeting, inviting every member of the commune to participate by voice and vote. In such meetings the majority vote decided all matters under discussion.

Aaron, an outstanding personality in Brotherly Labor, served as the main sheepherder. His Jewish background led him to choose to follow the example Moses set when he tended his father-in-law's sheep. Aaron always dressed in a long toga, held in place by a belt. He grew an impressively long beard and walked with a shepherd's crook in his hand.

Strict rules governed the commune. The "forbidden" list included the drinking of alcohol, the use of tobacco, and the singing of questionable songs. In summer the workday for all able-bodied persons lasted from sunrise to sunset; in winter, as the need demanded. A bell regulated the whole day's schedule: it sounded the hour for rising, for breakfast, dinner, midday snack, supper, and evening snack. And finally, it signaled the hour to retire.

The members divided the work according to ability, and need determined the size of the reward. The commune reserved any surplus for unexpected needs and for charity to be distributed as the general meetings saw fit. According to the regulations members of the commune were free to leave at any time, and the commune reserved the right to expel persons for specified reasons. Carefully worked rules determined the amount of money the commune permitted members to take with them when they left, but very few left. When they did, others took their places. The commune numbered 300 at the time it was disbanded in the late twenties.

Adventist Religion Practiced

The whole commune observed Saturday, the seventh day of the week, as the weekly holy day. It began Friday evening at the time the first star appeared and lasted until sunset Saturday evening. No unnecessary work went on during these 24 hours, and everyone seemed to enjoy the religious services that day.

Since Sundaykeepers surrounded Brotherly Labor, the members avoided doing any work on that day that might offend their neighbors. Instead they invited the neighbors to Bible studies or public meetings, which many attended.

The kitchen workers carefully followed biblical instruction as to clean and unclean foods (Lev. 11); no pork or other meat considered inedible found its way to the tables. Vegetables, fruits, dairy products, beef, eggs, and fish abounded on the farm. For the few vegetarians in the commune, the kitchen prepared special meals.

We do not know exactly how many other Adventist communal farms operated during the "golden decade," but reports refer to some of them. When H. J. Loebsack visited the Crimea in 1927 he mentioned a smaller communal farm near the city of Simferopol, close to the railway stations of Dsjankai and Taganasch.[4]

Twelve poor Adventist families numbering 40 persons received farmland from the government and operated a collective farm named Novy Put ("New Way"). They considered the main grainfield common property and worked it together, sharing the income. Each one received according to his contribution, either in labor or draft animals. In addition, each family owned its own house and a private garden plot. Evidently native Russians and Russians of German descent lived in this commune, for Loebsack writes that he conducted meetings there in both Russian and German.

After visiting there, Loebsack made an appeal to the General Conference for a tractor. This small community needed it not only for cultivating the soil but also for the irrigation pumps, threshing machines, and other things. Loebsack specified these needs to the authorities in the Soviet Union and obtained an import license dated March 19, 1928. Then through the General Conference he ordered a 10- to 20-horsepower tractor and a plow with three plowshares. Wisely he included in the request a complete set of spare parts for both. The General Conference agreed and arranged through the representative of the Soviet Union in New York to ship the farm implements to the Crimea. We note with interest this first and only time the world church and Communists cooperated in the operation of a communal farm.

On another occasion, Loebsack traveled to Tashkent in central Asia and made a trip into the Khirgiz Mountains. On the last leg of the trip he rode 40 miles with a team of horses to a place named Orlov. In these isolated areas he found colonies of Mennonites who had settled high up in the mountains seeking safety from Antichrist, whom they had expected in 1844. Among them Loebsack found 130 Seventh-day Adventists.

They lived far from any city, so the farmers experienced difficulties disposing of their milk products. In order to solve this problem the Adventists organized a cooperative that operated three cheese factories. They found it easy to sell their Russian-produced "Dutch" cheese to the population.

In the fertile Ukraine, Adventists operated several communal farms; one of them in the Dnepropetrovsk was named The Kingdom of Light and another Brotherly Love.

The City of the Sun

Although they never came to fruition, the magnificent plans for Solncegrad (City of the Sun) illustrate the thinking and hopes of evangelicals at this period in Communist rule. The unique idea originated in the fruitful mind of the Russian genius Ivan Stepanovich Prokhanov (1869-1935). Taking advantage of his expertise as an engineer, the American firm Westinghouse employed him to establish their plant in Petersburg. His brilliant mind, theological training, and knowledge of engineering, plus a strong personality, made him the natural choice as chairman of the Evangelical Christian All-Union Council. Under his outstanding leadership this organization, like the Seventh-day Adventists, established several evangelical communes carrying such biblical names as The Morning Star, Bethany, and Gethsemane. In the Caucasus the Pentecostals operated a farm called the Commune of the Apocalypse. But all these faded beside Prokhanov's brilliant plan for City of the Sun.

The plans called for a population of 800,000 Christians, so he needed a large piece of land. First he tried to obtain property in the south, but he failed to get support from the local authorities. Finally he focused on a large area of virgin soil in Asia in the Altai, at the confluence of the Biya and Katun rivers. On September 11, 1927, two representatives from the Evangelical Christian All-Union Council met with local authorities to inaugurate the venture with the solemn planting of oak trees. A detailed description of the plan appeared in the newspapers. A huge open space nearly one and a half miles in diameter formed the center. Here Prokhanov planned to plant many trees and build schools, hospitals, and houses of prayer. From the central area the drawings showed streets fanning out like the rays of the sun.[5]

No one questioned the feasibility of the undertaking. Prokhanov actually secured grants from an American Baptist named Rockefeller, money that was later used for other purposes. The Christian communal organizations had demonstrated the ability of Christian leaders to operate big businesses. But the authorities could not tolerate such a huge theocracy functioning like a separate island in a sea of Communism. Top Soviet officials intervened and the People's Commissariat of Agriculture, which favored the idea in the beginning, withdrew its support. That marked the end of Prokhanov's great plans. He lost courage and left the country, never to return. He died in Berlin with no pro-Soviet illusions.

Forced collectivization and accusations of religious propaganda in the sectarian communes signaled the end of the unique experiment with Christian communal farms in the Soviet Union. By the early thirties all of them had disintegrated and disappeared.

11 Two Congresses Debate Sensitive Issues

Non-Adventist publications and certain individuals within the Adventist Church in Western countries have published quite a bit about schisms in the Russian Adventist church. They concentrate especially on an offshoot movement that began more than half a century ago. On the other hand, leading Adventist papers contain little about this part of the church's experience. Let us examine the facts as far as we know them to find out what really happened.

We cannot deny that a split did occur and that it hurt the church. Political circumstances isolated church leaders and members in Russia from the world Seventh-day Adventist body during much of this period, and this made disagreements within the country worse. For decades the situation in the world barred General Conference administrators from working effectively with the leaders of the different factions and giving them unbiased counsel.

When conditions changed and the authorities granted permission for visiting church leaders to meet with key local persons to dig into the problems, together they found workable solutions. It did not happen overnight, but personal contacts, intensive committee work, and appeals to large congregations over a period of a few years eventually bore fruit. Russian Adventists today thank the Lord for a new spirit of unity. But we cannot understand the present unless we look at some illuminating events of the past.

1924 Adventist Congress Enjoys New Freedom

The Fifth All-Russian Congress of the Seventh-day Adventist Church mentioned earlier, met in Moscow from August 16 to 23, 1924, under the chairmanship of H. J. Loebsack. The leaders chose the opening date to coincide with the fortieth anniversary of the beginning of Adventist work in Russia, and the organization of the first church a little later in 1886. But Adventists remember the congress not so much for this celebration as for an action that caused much misunderstanding.

The congress met in a former Orthodox seminary that now serves as the official Third House of the Soviets. The authorities placed the building at the disposal of the delegates at half the cost usually charged to other conventions. Here they not only had their meeting rooms but also their sleeping quarters. The kitchen served food at reasonable prices. L. R. Conradi arrived in Moscow a few days after the congress ended and stayed in the same place. He comments that in his 26-bed room, planks had replaced spring mattresses, but he slept well, for everything was neat and clean.

The membership, at that time totaling about 12,000, sent representatives from such widely separated places as Siberia, Turkestan, North and Trans Caucasia, the Crimea, the Ukraine, and the regions around Lake Ladoga. According to Conradi, 105 delegates attended, but the minutes show that only 80 delegates signed the actions.

A large red banner on the front of the building advertised the congress, and newspapers carried reports of the proceedings. Many visitors attended the evening meetings, which were open to the public. Most surprising of all, on Sabbath the church conducted a large baptismal service in one of Moscow's beautiful suburban parks. The scenery reminded one writer of the River Jordan's banks. Hundreds of Moscovites viewed with great interest this unusual event, at which 53 persons confessed their faith through biblical baptism. Evidently this open practice of an important church rite created no problems, because two weeks later 14 additional persons symbolically buried their sins through baptism in this same place. Beautiful choir music, in addition to the baptism itself, attracted the public.

Churches of other denominations also took advantage of the new freedom. One visitor paints the following picture: "In 1924 I found in city after city, and village after village, the Protestants out in the open. Everywhere in the bazaars, Evangelical and Baptist preachers were holding forth on the meaning of their faith, unmolested either by Soviets or Communists. Sometimes they were heckled fiercely. But that neither dismayed nor disturbed them. If they were challenged to public debates, unlike Orthodox clergymen who often refused to meet revolutionaries in open discussion, they joyously accepted such challenges. Russia at that time teemed with talk of religion, and public debates on the subject were more common than motion pictures, were indeed one of the chief intellectual diversions and indoor sports of the masses." [1] The writer also mentions as a typical example of the freedom of the time, that in the city of Stalingrad, the Soviet allowed a Baptist minister free use of the city theater on Sunday afternoons.

Keep in mind this new and promising background of religious liberty as we examine a much-disputed message the congress sent to the government.

The Declaration Sent to Government

The delegates to the congress voted and signed what they called a Declaration Regarding the Principles of Faith and Organization of Seventh-day Adventists and sent it to the Central Executive Committee of the Soviet Union. The first part dealt with facts about the church, how it operated worldwide, and statistics of the church within the Soviet Union. It then mentioned its relationship to the state in these words:

"Seventh-day Adventists give expression to the respect in

which they hold the organizers of the [Soviet] Union who have secured us political as well as religious freedom and declare it necessary that we fulfill our duty to the state, social as well as military. With satisfaction have we hailed the decree published on the fourth of January 1919 and reaffirmed on the twentieth of December 1920, a decree which is the only one of its kind in the world, and worthy of imitation by all nations. [This decree exempted persons from military service on religious grounds.] It shows us that the Union government is actively engaged in securing us full liberty of conscience, in that it allows us to fulfill our duty to the state in accordance with our conscientious convictions before God, and before the Union government as well.

"The doctrines of Seventh-day Adventists allow them liberty of conscience on the point and prescribe to them no rule of action, seeing that in the matter of military service every person, according to his private conviction, stands himself responsible, and the Conference does not prevent such members to serve in the front service, if their conscience allows them. Whatever service one undertakes, should, as a citizen's duty, be conscientiously discharged.

"Basing our opinion on the principles of divine world government, we feel convinced that in the providence of God, the heart of our unforgettable V. I. Lenin has been guided, and wisdom been vouchsafed upon him and the near circle of his colaborers for the creation of the only progressive government machine, fitting the times, the world has to show."

The declaration goes on to list the wishes of Seventh-day Adventists, such as personal religious liberty and freedom to print literature, establish hospitals, and travel abroad. It promises cooperation in building up the state and expresses a desire to be "a rose in the bouquet of believing citizens of the Socialist Union Republic." [2]

The managing committee of the congress—H. J. Loebsack, J. A. Ljow, G. T. Zierat, W. S. Dyman, W. G. Tarazowsky—

and 75 other delegates signed the document. They made no secret of the declaration, for they printed 5,000 copies and spread it widely not only in Russia and Europe but as far away as South Africa.

Naturally, the statement labeling Communist rule as "the only progressive government machine, fitting the times, the world has to show" met opposition outside Russia. A similar statement about any political rule anywhere in the world, regardless of how benign its government might appear to those making it, would undoubtedly also provoke disagreement. In this case, observers today often forget that the only other rule the Russians knew from personal experience was the church/state suppression under the czars. At that time the Communist rule contrasted favorably with the former. The Communists released religious dissenters from prisons and labor camps, separated the state from the church, permitted religious propaganda, and exempted religious conscientious objectors from armed military service. The hardships of the thirties and late fifties were still in the future.

The other part of the declaration that raised questions was the portion referring to Adventist members and military service: "The Conference does not prevent such members to serve in the front service, if their conscience allows them."

In order to understand this action it is essential to remember that the Leninist decree granting exemption from military service to conscientious objectors was still in force. (The state abolished it two years later on August 2, 1926, after Lenin's death.) The remarkable decree bore this title: "Decree of the Soviet People's Commissars, 4 January 1919, on Exemption From Military Service on Religious Grounds."

The first paragraph stated: "Persons who are unable to serve in the armed forces because of their religious beliefs are to be given the right (by decision of a People's Court) to alternative service for the same period as their contemporaries: in medical services, primarily in hospitals for contagious diseases, or in correspondingly socially useful work, at the choice of the conscript himself.'' [3]

The third paragraph even stated that if the alternatives also proved incompatible with particular religious convictions, such persons could be completely free from all civil duties! [4] Seen against this background we can better understand why Adventists praised government rule as ''the best in the world.'' Even V. A. Shelkov, who criticized the main body of Seventh-day Adventists for their attitude to this issue, approvingly quotes Lenin's words: ''Let us adopt this decree to calm down and satisfy those who have already borne dreadful torments and persecution from the czarist government.''

During World War I most drafted Adventists found that the government practiced to a great degree what the Exemption Decree permitted. H. J. Loebsack, wrote to the General Conference session of 1922:

''At the beginning of the war, the brethren who had been drafted came to us and asked what they should do. Were they to take up arms against their conscience, or were they to allow themselves to be killed by those who did? We who have endeavored to train our people to be self-reliant and to develop their individual responsibility toward God, to their conscience, and the state, could not prescribe what they should do or what they would have to consider as proper and their duty at the post assigned to them. Only He who has created them had the right to command and the power to protect them. They made their own decisions; and the majority of the brethren, numbering some 500, with many of our workers, were assigned the sanitary and other noncombatant service.'' [5]

With such experiences behind them and in view of the exemption decree, Loebsack and the other delegates indeed saw reasons to praise the government in these matters and to recommend that drafted personnel follow their conscientious conviction on military questions. Their recommendations in 1924 do not differ much from the present attitude of the world church on this point. Charles Martin, director of the National Service Organization of the General Conference of Seventh-day Adventists, expressed a similar opinion to the world's leading magazine on religious liberty. He states:

"The attitude of the Christian should always be of loyalty to his government. . . . But when the government conflicts with the requirements of God, he must obey God, at whatever cost."

He then refers to Bible texts dealing with the question, both the commandment not to kill and on the other side, the God-given power of government. He closes with these words: *"The Adventist Church recommends that its youth, if drafted, enter the forces as noncombatants. But the church also recognizes the right of individual conscience. An Adventist bearing arms is in no way a second-class church member. In some countries, no provision is made for noncombatants; there Adventist soldiers may carry guns."* [6]

At the next nationwide Adventist congress, four years later, the delegates took a completely different course. An action voted then probably caused more furor among Adventists than anything else that has happened in Russia.

1928 Congress Makes Questionable Decision

The Sixth Seventh-day Adventist All-Union Federal Congress convened in Moscow from May 12 to 19, 1928. Eighty-three delgates came from all parts of the country and were selected on the basis of one for each union organization and one for each 200 members. No representative from the General Conference attended, so again no influence from outside affected the proceedings. The following served as chairmen: H. J. Loebsack, J. A. Ljwow, J. J. Wilson; P. A. Swiridow and A. Ausin served as secretaries.

This time the congress met in the Peter and Paul Orthodox Cathedral, which evangelical Christians were using for their services. The congress needed this large church building because more than 500 Adventists joined the Sabbath meetings from the five churches functioning in Moscow. The evening meetings, open to the public, were attended by more than 1,000 persons.

Encouraging reports highlighted improved opportunities for church activities. When the congress had met in 1924, the authorities still forbade the church to print literature, so typists produced both the Sabbath school quarterlies and Week of Prayer readings on 14 typewriters, making 10 carbon copies at a time. Imagine the impossible task of providing sufficient copies for 13,303 members! But now the church printed two Russian and one German monthly paper; quarterlies, which they called "Bible Proofs;" and Week of Prayer Readings, also in Russian and German. In addition they had printed a Russian Bible, a hymnal with music, and a large poster of the Ten Commandments. This poster, framed, still decorates the walls of several Adventist churches today. They had also received permission to import German, Lithuanian, and Estonian Bibles.

The congress ordained eight ministers: six Russians, one German, and one Lithuanian. This indicated the growing strength of the Russian work, in contrast to early efforts that mainly were among people of German extraction.

The delegates unanimously voted the following action, which later created quite a stir: "Based on the teachings of Holy Scripture in the Old and New Testament (1 Samuel 8:10-12; 10:25; Luke 20:25; Romans 13:1-6; Titus 3:1), which say that the rule of the government has been designed by God as an institution to punish evil and to protect the pious, and in view of the Declaration of the Fifth Seventh-day Adventist Congress, in which our relationship to the Soviet Government has been clearly stated, the Sixth Federal Congress decided that Seventh-day Adventists have the duty to render unto Caesar that which is Caesar's and to God that which is God's. That is, to perform any governmental and military service in all of its forms according to the basic constitution, which is valid for all citizens. Each one who teaches a different doctrine and who asks for the nonfulfillment of their duty towards the government, the congress considers a heretic who separates himself from the teachings of the Holy Scriptures and from the unity of God's church, and therefore places himself outside of the Seventh-day Adventist organization." [7]

This statement deviates radically from general Adventist understanding of the church's relationship to members who refuse to serve in the military—an understanding that has changed little during the past six decades. In 1920 A. G. Daniells, then president of the General Conference of the Seventh-day Adventist Church, made statements similar to those made by Charles Martin quoted above. Speaking to German leaders, Daniells said: "After careful study we came to the conclusion that as a church we believe and accept the principle of noncombatancy." But he also added "We must, however, permit every member of our country to follow his own conscience and decide himself what his position with reference to the government should be. We have not disfellowshipped a single one of these members because of their different stand on this subject, and we have not treated a single one of them as though he were not a Christian." [8]

The action taken by the Moscow Congress in 1928, describing as "heretics" and "outside the Seventh-day Adventist organization" those who refused to do military service, cannot be considered as representing a valid Adventist position.

Shadows Darken Bright Days

Available Russian church documents do not reveal what led the 1928 congress to place in its minutes this statement that obviously neither the world church at large nor its leaders supported. We do know that the church leaders in Russia were of solid faith, for shortly after the congress they faced prison and death courageously. Perhaps in some way the foreshadowing of those situations influenced their judgment—or there may have been other unknown influences.

The *Seventh-day Adventist Encyclopedia* points out that at the beginning of 1929 "there was a marked change in the government's policy toward religion." The new restrictions forbade ministers to visit isolated members, limited them to a local congregation, and made them accountable for the political reliability of each member. Other restrictions brought the printing of literature to a stop and caused untold sufferings to Adventists through enforced collectivization and demands to work on Saturdays. Some farmers could not obtain other work and starved to death. The five-day workweek with the sixth day off made it impossible for Adventists to work in large factories. This arrangement was in force from 1929 to 1940.

About 1930 the government dissolved all the conferences, and in the following purges the police arrested and exiled many ministers and members. Some lost their lives. Soon all members of the All-Union Committee languished in exile or prison. H. J. Loebsack went to prison and died a martyr's death in 1938, following four years of isolation in a lonely cell at the state prison Yaroslave. Reports reached the outside world that no Adventist congregational worship functioned in the whole country.[9]

Did these approaching events overshadow the congress? Did outside forces influence and perhaps even decide what went into the minutes? Statements by persons who lived there at the time and who closely followed the events indicate that such was the case. The action about military service, which so drastically differed from earlier instruction by the same leaders who chaired the 1924 congress, raises questions, of course. In spite of the proclaimed "unanimous" vote, suspicion and doubt as to its origin spread and contributed to the divisions discussed in the next chapter.

12

A Serious Split
Threatens the Church

The Adventist Church has joined forces with fallen Babylon! Leave her!'' This accusation and appeal originated in Germany in 1914 and created a movement small in number but far-reaching in influence. It spread to several countries; minor groups still exist in Europe, and there is even a small group in the United States. Russia did not escape. One of the key criticisms targeted German church leaders' attitude toward armed service and Sabbathkeeping in the army. Adherents also claimed to follow strictly the Spirit of Prophecy teachings, in contrast, as they saw it, to the church at large.

Reformism Reaches Russia

Two believers in Leningrad, E. Remmer and C. Nitevich, contacted one of the reformist leaders in Germany, Heinrich Spanknoebel. He sent them printed promotional materials that soon reached areas far removed from Leningrad. In 1926 G. Zirat, Ukrainian Union president, wrote to W. A. Spicer: ''The so-called Reformists have disturbed some of the churches in Turkestan. They quote statements from the Testimonies that are available only in English, which they claim prove that before her death Sister White declared the General Conference leaders apostate and rejected. They have compiled a whole book consisting of quotations from the Testimonies and sent it here from Germany. You know this movement, but here it is something new, and it creates a bad spirit.'' [1]

Two years later the Adventist congress in Moscow voted a warning against an "organization which has departed from us as mentioned in Acts 20:30 and 1 John 2:19. Therefore we recommend to all our members: Separate yourselves from the false Reformists who wrongly call themselves The Seventh-day Adventist Reform Movement. They are led astray by false concepts of godly living and cause division among the fold of Christ." [2]

This action shows that the 1928 congress in Moscow did not cause the Russian offshoot movement. It already existed as an organization when the congress convened.

These Reformists, which, like their German counterparts, considered the official Adventist Church as apostatized, operated first under G. Ostwald as leader. In 1936 they changed their name to the All-Union Center of Reform Adventists, and P. A. Manjlera and V. A. Shelkov shared in the leadership. During the difficult years that began in the early thirties, many ministers from both the official Adventist Church and the Reformists suffered severely. Some lost their lives. Reformist leader V. A. Shelkov went through great hardships in labor camps and prisons. He spent 13 years in exile in Karaganda, in central Asia, and the Urals of Siberia. G. Ostwald died in prison, but Shelkov survived. Released in 1954, he took over as chairman and renamed the movement The True and Free Seventh-day Adventist, the name it still goes by today.

In his writings Shelkov reflects the influence from events that took place during World War I. He refers to statements made in 1914 by leaders he calls false Adventists and draws a parallel with the 1924 Declaration in Russia.[3] Typical also is correspondence from a Reformist pastor to relatives in the United States in which he claims that "Adventists apostatized in 1914, first in Germany through their leading brethren." Then he indicates that his Adventist relatives in America are part of Babylon: "You and many souls in your church are in apostasy, but it is because you do not know better." This attitude corresponds to statements made to me in personal discussions with some Reformist members in the U.S.S.R.

But why do they condemn the whole world church? One argument is that General Conference president A. G. Daniells, at a meeting in Friedensau, Germany, July 21 to 23, 1920, supported a statement made by German leaders to their government in 1914 to the effect that they would bear arms and serve on the Sabbath. But the stenographic transcript of those meetings proves just the opposite. Daniells expressed regret and disagreement with some of their statements, but as we noted in the last chapter, he also stressed the freedom of each individual to follow his conscientious convictions.

Another argument they make is that at the 1922 world session in San Francisco Daniells supported the German position. But the minutes of the session mention nothing of such approval, either by the president or anyone else. And no action was taken on that matter.

International Attention Focuses on Shelkov

Vladimir Andreevich Shelkov (1895-1980) unquestionably ranks as the best-known person ever to belong to the Seventh-day Adventist Church in Russia. Although his movement was never large in numbers, international press and religious journals around the world abound with reports about him and his followers. Why did they pinpoint this leader and group more than any other in the Soviet Union? Perhaps Shelkov's prolific writings provide a partial answer to the question. He authored eight books under the general title *The Just War for Freedom of Conscience Against the Dictatorship of Atheism*. Keston College in England lists 22 other titles in their possession, which include sermons, doctrinal statements, historic studies of Adventism, and biblical tracts.[4]

Shelkov's secret publishing house, The True Witness, printed his productions, and a network of underground channels spread them all over the country. Copies appear in such widely separated areas as the Baltic, central Asia, Siberia, and the Far East.

His dramatic life story intrigued foreign correspondents, who met from time to time with representatives of the True and Free Seventh-day Adventists. They played up the fact that in 1945 a court sentenced Shelkov to death, and only after he had spent two months on death row did it change the sentence to 10 years' imprisonment. He was in and out of labor camps and prisons until his total incarceration time amounted to 23 years!

When finally freed, he decided to live in hiding, but he continued his ceaseless activities. He established close links with the Soviet human rights movements, and contacted academician Andrei Sakharov. Shelkov also wrote to President Jimmy Carter, appealing for help in securing the release of Alexander Ginzburg.

On March 14, 1978, the police arrested Shelkov for the fifth time, at the home of his daughter, Dina Lepshin, in Tashkent. Andrei Sakharov tried to attend the trial, but police denied him access to the courtroom. The sentence on March 29, 1979, shocked the world: five years in a strict-regime labor camp. For an old man of 83, this was tantamount to a death sentence. Sakharov appealed for help to the pope and heads of the states that had signed the Helsinki Agreement. Again Shelkov captured the eyes of the world, but in vain. He died in a Siberian labor camp on January 27, 1980.

At the world meeting in Madrid, Spain (1980), where 35 governments took part in the Conference on Security and Cooperation in Europe, Shelkov's movement again caught the international limelight. The conference reviewed how each signatory nation had kept to the Helsinki agreement of 1975, which deals with "respect for human rights and fundamental freedoms, including the freedom of thought, conscience, and religion or belief." The True and Free Adventists managed to smuggle out of the Soviet Union an 863-page report dealing with their experiences and charging that the Soviet Union violated the Helsinki Agreement. Of course, the international group of journalists who were present dispatched news of this all over the world.

While visiting Samarkand in central Asia in 1984, I spent an evening with Shelkov's daughter Rimina and her husband, Oleg Tvetskov. They live in the outskirts of Tashkent in a house that belonged to Shelkov. Oleg Tsvetskov spent 15 years of his life in prisons and labor camps because of his close collaboration with his father-in-law. He shared eight of his prison years with Shelkov and knew him as intimately as did his daughter. Both have now disassociated themselves from the True and Free Adventists.

What is the membership of this group? Nobody knows the exact figures, because they meet in secret and obviously do not provide membership lists. During the past few years, however, some of Shelkov's supporters from different republics in the U.S.S.R. have returned to the Seventh-day Adventist Church. Adding up the information from these persons and other sources, the highest possible figure for 1985 did not exceed 3,000, and may be even less.

The Main Adventist Body Faces a Split

Shelkov and his followers "developed a clear political aim, that of a secular state which exercises no ideological influence." [5] But they failed to attract a greater number of Adventists in spite of the fact that many might sympathize with their opposition to armed service and their strict Sabbath observance. But few solid believers subscribed to their notion that the Adventist Church forms part of Babylon and they should come out of it. Most Adventists also distanced themselves from Shelkov's political involvement.

But soon another budding organization looked more attractive because it did not attack the world movement that Adventists in general love and defend. A look at the political situation helps us understand what took place in the church.

111

While Communist Party chief Nikita Khrushchev (who ruled from 1953 to 1964) showed a comparatively tolerant attitude toward Christian believers during his first years in power, he soon changed. In the late fifties he decided to stamp out religion, and boasted that by 1965 religion would become obsolete. "When that happens," he joked, "I will insist that at least one Christian be preserved and placed in a museum so that future generations of Soviets can view an extinct species!"

Of course his prophecy failed, but much suffering and severe restrictions harmed believers until his fellow Communists ousted him in 1964. During this difficult time the last vestige of official Adventist organization disappeared. A government decree in December 1960 dissolved the Seventh-day Adventist All-Union Council, led by S. P. Kulysshki. Thirty years earlier the state had closed all conferences and unions, leaving only individual churches to function legally.

Under such circumstances it is no wonder that schisms began to develop in the church! Gradually two factions developed. One of them, with M. P. Kulakov emerging as leader, decided to make the best of the situation by cooperating with the authorities as far as possible. They registered their churches, operated legally, and met in designated places. A. Demidov, Kulakov's uncle and once editor of the Adventist journal *Golos Istiny* ("Voice of Truth") published in Moscow from 1925 to 1929, perhaps best expressed the reasons and purpose for this policy. During my conversations with him in Moscow he repeated the same sentiments he once wrote:

"We [Adventists] must search and find something in common with the atheists in Communist Russia; as the divinely established church in the midst of the raging ocean of socialistic all-pervading atheism, we must not permit ourselves to be swallowed up in it, and we must not refuse to search until we find something that we have in common with unbelievers. Our mission is to carry the gospel invitation 'to every nation, and kindred, and tongue, and people.' 'Every' includes also the atheistic, unbelieving Communist sector of the world. In order to accomplish this we must not stress those things that *divide* us from these builders of the new social order, but rather those things which *unite* us with them.''

Demidov agrees with the Communist criticism of Christianity as the ally, historically, of capitalism and imperialism. Writing about the church in general, he further states: ''The church, which has become organically one with despotism and capitalism, . . . has trampled upon the rights of entire nations and of the laboring man.'' [6]

The other faction generally (but not in every case) refused registration and opposed all interference by the authorities; they often arranged their meetings without seeking permission to do so. P. A. Mazanow, president of the Seventh-day Adventist All-Union Council from 1952 to 1954, was the leading personality in this group. He is one of the few, and perhaps the only one, among present Adventist leaders to receive an Adventist education. Like Kulakov, he speaks several languages. When, for instance, the Southern European Union treasurer R. Gerber visited the U.S.S.R. in 1956, he preached in German with Mazanow translating. Within both groups some families sent their children to school on Sabbaths and some did not.

In the more relaxed atmosphere that followed Khrushchev's effort to crush the churches, Mazanow chaired a meeting in Kiev in January of 1965, which 180 pastors attended. They decided to found a new central body, the Council of Senior Brethren, with Mazanow as leader. The fact that Kulakov's father became a member of the board illustrates the depth of the split. He later detached himself from it.

The division soon reached serious proportions. When I visited the country a few years after the Kiev meeting, I found that the split deeply divided friends and families. On Sabbath mornings some went to church in one part of the city while others attended services at the same time in another part of the

AIR-8

city. Accusations of "stealing members" from each other created a miserable spirit.

Fundamental doctrines did not play any role in the schism, and both sides disassociated themselves from the True and Free Adventists. But under these circumstances, churches weakened and growth seemed impossible. The future looked bleak. Fortunately, things changed.

13

A New Day Dawns

The year following the visit, my wife and I made in 1977, another historic event took place for the Seventh-day Adventist Church in the Soviet Union. Robert H. Pierson, then president of the General Conference, had hoped for several years to meet with Adventists in the Soviet Union. On my journey I helped to lay the groundwork for such a visit. But not until August of 1978 were all the necessary formalities in place. Then he and I, with our wives, received visas with the magic words written in that designated us not as ordinary tourists but as official guests from the Seventh-day Adventist Church to the Union of Soviet Socialist Republics (U.S.S.R.). This type of visa made quite a difference for this and succeeding visits.

On our arrival at Moscow's international airport, a man with an air of authority about him slapped special labels on our suitcases. They bore three large letters, VIP, in striking red and blue colors. From that moment on we had no delays at customs with regard to papers or luggage. I still possess these labels, perhaps with the faint hope that they might be useful again, somewhere, sometime. At least they make nice souvenirs! Everyone we dealt with did his best to make things easy and to make us feel welcome.

A large, elegant limousine with a chauffeur took us from one appointment to another during the entire period of our stay in Moscow. We made good use of it to get to preaching services, committee appointments, banquets, private homes, and to government offices for discussions with officials. At each place the driver waited for us—sometimes for hours. We learned to appreciate his expertise in the crowded streets of the city, although at times we felt he aimed at "flying low" rather than just driving fast. But we liked him, and he seemed to like us. He commented to one of the brethren, "I like the Seven-day people. They do not swear, are never drunk, and are always friendly."

But the friendliness of the people and the comforts so thoughtfully provided did not mean our visit was a vacation. Since we wanted to accomplish as much good as possible, we kept busy every moment of every day and far into the night. A leading pastor expressed it well when he showed us our daily schedule and remarked, "We will take good care of you. We will put you in the best hotels available, serve you plenty of food, and use the most efficient transportation, but we will squeeze you like a lemon!"

A group in the city of Tula highlighted the reason for making every moment of this unique visit count. The woman who prepared the meals for the group of young men working on the construction of the church baked a delicious layer cake to celebrate Pierson's visit to their city Noticing a few Russian words written in chocolate on top of the cake, I asked what they meant. The reply: "It happens only once in a lifetime!"

Traveling by planes, trains, buses, and private cars, we went from Moscow to Tula to Sochi and Odessa. We visited Kiev in the Ukraine, Riga and Tallinn in the Baltic republics, and ended our tour in Leningrad. In each of these places are Seventh-day Adventist churches, and our VIP status as official visitors gave us free access to the pulpits. It also included permission for the church to provide travel tickets and pay for the hotels, and they insisted on doing this.

Again Adventists came from far and near, realizing that this opportunity to see and hear a General Conference president might indeed happen only "once in a lifetime." In every city we spoke to large audiences, visited homes, had conversations with workers, met with public officials, and took time for interviews with journalists and radio reporters. Everything took place within the narrow time frame of three weeks. This made for extremely long days and short nights. But it all added up to a happy and memorable experience.

We enjoyed our visit to the beautiful city of Odessa, the leading Soviet port on the Black Sea. In spite of the thick ice of winter, Odessa Bay stays open all year with the help of heavy icebreakers. Our thriving membership meets in the Baptist church on Sabbaths. A large portion of the 1,500 people who attended our meetings here stood outside and listened to the sermons through loudspeakers. Although rain poured from a gray sky, nobody left early, not even those without umbrellas!

Adventists in the Soviet Union seem to live less-hurried lives than most of us in the West. This includes their worship services, especially on occasions such as this. "Preach for two or three hours as the Lord directs," the pastors advised. "The people are not in a hurry. They have come first of all to worship. You will disappoint them if you send them home too soon." Pierson gracefully accepted the challenge; in one place he preached what he said was the longest sermon of his entire ministry—it lasted for an hour and 50 minutes!

The Blessed Hope in the Baltic

In Tallinn, Estonia, another extraordinary Sabbath highlighted our journey. The Baptists, who, by the way, are the largest Protestant denomination in the Soviet Union and are growing steadily, now use St. Olaf's Cathedral. It formerly belonged to the Lutherans, most of them descendants of German emigrants. Many of them had moved back to Germany after World War II. The few who remained no longer needed such a large cathedral and do not possess adequate funds to maintain it. Therefore the authorities turned it over to the

Baptists, who kindly loaned the tradition-rich building to the Adventists for both their Friday evening and Sabbath services. Every one of the 1,500 seats was taken, and many listeners stood around the walls.

As in Moscow, Tula, Kiev, and other places, the music was inspiring. A mixed choir, a male chorus, duets, and rich instrumental numbers under the direction of talented musicians added blessings to the services. The music climaxed with an outstanding performance of Handel's "Hallelujah Chorus." some ask if Russian Adventists can present the truth of Christ's second coming in their churches. They certainly can. And nowhere do I find the "blessed hope" more dear to the members than there. In more than one place we heard choirs sing the beloved theme song from one of the General Conference sessions, "We Have This Hope." Here in Tallinn the choir sang it not only in Estonian but also in English, for our benefit. The text expresses beautifully the longing of every true Adventist:

> We have this hope that burns within our hearts,
> Hope in the coming of the Lord.
> We have this faith that Christ alone imparts,
> Faith in the promise of His Word.
> We believe the time is here,
> When the nations far and near
> Shall awake and shout and sing:
> Hallelujah! Christ is King!
> We have this hope that burns within our hearts,
> Hope in the coming of the Lord.

—Wayne Hooper, © 1962

Adventist Theology Survives

For many years the Adventist Church in the U.S.S.R. lived almost completely isolated from the mainstream of worldwide Adventism. Especially has this been true since the authorities dissolved all conferences and unions in the 1930s and only an

All-Union Committee with little or no administrative influence existed in Moscow. But in the hearts of Russian Adventists the love for the message in no way diminished. On the contrary, their faithfulness to God, the warmth of their fellowship, and their respect for the General Conference is greater than in many places. They adhere faithfully to Adventist doctrines. For them the Bible is indeed the Word of God, and they highly esteem counsel from the Spirit of Prophecy. As in the rest of the world, they raise questions on some matters and debate them, but no serious division of opinion exists regarding the "landmarks" and basic Adventist theology.

The influence of the Spirit of Prophecy helped the main church body to avoid the fanatacism that might so easily have crept in during the isolation. Modern editions of Ellen White's books printed in Russian do not exist, but I saw 50-year-old copies of books such as *The Great Controversy* and *The Desire of Ages* still in use, although almost falling to pieces. Many ministers own typed translations of these classics. *Steps to Christ* helped them to avoid the extremes of legalism on the one hand and cheap grace on the other. Soundly balanced statements such as the following from *Steps to Christ* helped believers to grasp the fundamental doctrine of righteousness by faith:

"There are two errors against which the children of God—particularly those who have just come to trust in His grace—need to guard. The first . . . is that of looking to their own works, trusting to anything they can do, to bring themselves into harmony with God. He who is trying to become holy by his own works in keeping the law, is attempting an impossibility. All that man can do without Christ is polluted with selfishness and sin. It is the grace of Christ alone, through faith, that can make us holy.

"The opposite and no less dangerous error is, that belief in Christ releases men from keeping the law of God; that since by faith alone we become partakers of the grace of Christ, our

119

works have nothing to do with our redemption. . . . "We do not earn salvation by our obedience; for our salvation is the free gift of God, to be received by faith. But obedience is the fruit of faith." *

Since they have very limited opportunities for printing literature, and nothing at all for mass distribution, Adventists have found other legal ways of providing material for spiritual guidance. With typewriters they type 10 readable carbon copies at a time. Several such typewritten books circulate. On one bookshelf I saw three large volumes of *The Seventh-day Adventist Bible Commentary,* New Testament portion, translated, beautifully typed, and bound.

Recently the authorities permitted Seventh-day Adventists to print 10,000 copies of the Bible on Soviet presses and to sell them to members. Since the special thin paper generally used for Bibles was not available then, these Bibles are large, easily weighing about four pounds each. But the print appears clear and easy to read, and the Bibles contain the complete word of God. In 1984 Adventists also printed 5,000 copies of the New Testament with the Psalms. Earlier, Baptists shared some of their Bibles with Adventists when they received permission to print an edition.

Twice a year the church prints 1,000 copies of a 100-page booklet. It includes the Week of Prayer readings, church news, and spiritual articles. For the first quarter of 1985, 1,000 quarterlies with 12 Bible studies in each came off the presses for the first time in many years. Three thousand copies of a Morning Watch Calendar, with 136 pages of short readings for each day of 1985, was another first. During the past few years, Soviet presses produced 15,000 hymnbooks, with 525 hymns, for Adventists. Five thousand included music, especially for choirs, and 10,000 were with text only.

Resources and tools such as these help to unify the church and build the faith of the members.

A Ministry of Healing

As we have seen, the mainstream of Seventh-day Adventism in the U.S.S.R. gradually developed a schism that weakened the witness of the church. Doctrinal differences did not cause it, but rather disagreement as to what adjustments to make under a radically changed social and political situation. Being cut off from the mediating influences of the world church as they were, we can imagine how misunderstandings between two main factions grew and dissension widened.

We must also keep in mind that no schools or seminaries for training workers exist, and no unifying literature could be printed and circulated to all the members. When opportunities for contacts and counsel with the General Conference opened up, world church leaders began quietly and patiently to draw people together in renewed bonds of love and fellowship.

Robert H. Pierson was able to make a great contribution to this healing process. Many others contributed to the measure of success achieved, but he brought the dissenting brethren face to face and convinced them of their desperate need to end the infighting. Russian and General Conference leaders staked out a course and laid a foundation for reconciliation and cooperation. Each visit I made during the succeeding years convinced me of the lasting results of Pierson's visit.

Pierson's sermons on salvation in Christ, unity in the faith, and the power of the Advent message went from his heart to the hearts of his many listeners. Recorded on tape and copied and played again and again all over the U.S.S.R., his every word reached thousands. The power of the Holy Spirit touched the hearts of pastors and lay people and often resulted in moving expressions of sorrow for past mistakes and both personal and public appeals for forgiveness. When strong men burst into tears and embraced in the pulpit and pledged cooperation, hundreds wept with them and thanked the Lord for the dawning of a new day. This deep stirring of feelings did not solve all the problems that had accumulated through long years, but it marked a vital beginning. During the years since then it has been my privilege to follow up and try to nurture and reinforce the good resolutions. Several other visitors from the General Conference played a vital role as they assisted in this work.

14 Building Bridges

I n 1981 Neal C. Wilson and his wife visited the Soviet Union, and Mrs. Lohne and I accompanied them. Robert Pierson had retired from the presidency of the Seventh-day Adventist world organization, and Wilson had succeeded him. Again large crowds gathered to meet the visitors from the General Conference. According to estimates, about 6,000 people attended the various services on the weekdays and three weekends we spent in the U.S.S.R. The large number of people present and the long distances they traveled proved that pastors and church leaders gave wide publicity to this special visit.

Largest country in the world, the Soviet Union with its 8.6 million square miles covers an even greater land area than did the Roman Empire at the peak of its strength. In population, only China and India have more people than the 272 million plus who live in the Soviet Union. The distance between its eastern and western borders measures 6,800 miles and spans 11 time zones. This means that as twilight fades into darkness at one edge of the country, dawn breaks at the other. Morning and evening occur at the same time in the same country!

Through repeated visits during the past 16 years I have learned to know many Adventists personally. At the first weekend of the 1981 visit, in the Baptist church building in Moscow, I recognized well-known and loved faces among the packed congregation. I saw friends from such widely separated areas as Moldavia, near Romania; Tula, in the Russian Soviet Federated Socialist Republic; Kiev, in the heart of the Ukraine; and Armenia, by the Caspian Sea. They also came from Alma-Ata, near China, and from many other places. They came to hear God's word, to listen to fine choirs and musical groups, and to enjoy fellowship with other members. And this time they came especially to meet the new world leader of the Seventh-day Adventist Church, Neal Wilson.

Bridging the Gulf

What should be the church's relationship to government authorities? We have seen that in the Soviet Union this question created differences of opinion. Some churches sought official registration and received permission to organize and conduct services in certain buildings at specific times. Others did not seek this contact. They not only did not register but also did not ask formal permission for their meetings.

Generally speaking, the practice Seventh-day Adventists follow all over the world is founded on two biblical principles. The first they base on Romans 13:1, 2: "Let every person be subject to the governing authorities. For there is no authority except from God, and those that exist have been instituted by God. Therefore he who resists the authorities resists what God has appointed" (RSV).

The other principle, taken from Acts 5:29, tells how far this subjection should go: "We must obey God rather than men." Matthew 22:21 expresses the same thought: "Render therefore to Caesar the things that are Caesar's, and to God the things that are God's." Our advice to the Russian churches and leaders during several visits has constantly been to follow the guidelines in these Bible texts. The unity that now exists regarding the question of relationship to the authorities rests on these principles. The guidelines do not, of course, exclude the fact that the individual himself must make certain decisions, only after consulting his own conscience.

Prior to our 1981 visit, Neal Wilson and I sent a pastoral letter to the churches in the Soviet Union. The following is a quotation from that letter:

"From time to time questions are raised as to the attitude of the General Conference toward believers and their church organizations in countries where it has not been possible to follow in detail the organizational procedures Seventh-day Adventists have outlined in their Church Manual and Working Policy. To this we answer that the following principles should be practiced and serve as a guide in such situations:

"1. The General Conference can recognize only one Seventh-day Adventist organization in any country. This would normally be the one recognized by the authorities. We conduct our work in harmony with biblical principles expressed in texts such as Romans 13:1-8 and Acts 5:29. On this basis we encourage all who consider themselves to be Seventh-day Adventists to identify with the recognized body of believers. We are convinced that this is in harmony with biblical and Spirit of Prophecy counsel to the church.

"2. The General Conference recognizes that in some countries there are divisions of opinion among those who profess to be good and faithful Seventh-day Adventists. Usually these differences of opinion do not relate to fundamental doctrinal matters, but rather as to how individuals understand and practice Bible instruction such as 'Render therefore unto Caesar the things which are Caesar's; and unto God the things that are God's' (Matt. 22:21). We honor the conscience of each believer in this respect and reach out with brotherly love and pastoral concern to all who accept Christ as Lord and who want to obey God's commandments and be considered members of the spiritual body of Seventh-day Adventist believers.

"3. The General Conference appeals to those who hold differing opinions to talk to and fellowship with each other in love and with mutual respect. Fellow believers should avoid attitudes, actions, and words that misrepresent the church and tend to create unholy strife among believers.

"In all this we aim for unity in Christ, oneness in faith and practice, and, hopefully, eventual union in one church organization." *

To our great joy we found that years of working with individuals, discussion with representatives from the two main sides, and appeals to large audiences had not been in vain. Influential leaders in the church, M. P. Kulakov, N. A. Zhukaluk, D. A. Grenz, R. N. Volkoslaviski, M. S. Zazulin, I. F. Parachuk, A. F. Parasey, N. N. Libenko, and many others too numerous to name, had a great part in bringing the factions together. Without their positive attitude, no one from outside could have accomplished much.

When we met in Moscow this time, leaders from both sides made it clear right from the beginning that they came determined to work together. Under Wilson's able leadership, the two factions reached a substantial degree of agreement. Open discussions built new bridges of understanding and confirmed the willingness to cooperate that three of the key leaders, M. P. Kulakov, M. S. Zazulin, and I. F. Parachuk, had expressed to me the year before.

Two years later, G. Ralph Thompson, secretary of the General Conference, wrote: "I can testify that the merger of the two groups has worked successfully. I met with them and heard their testimony; I saw Christian brother sitting next to Christian brother, smiling and hugging each other, telling me how a few years before they did not speak to one another. Seeing such evidence of God's power, I praised Him for His ability to heal the wounds of misunderstanding." Repentance for past mistakes, intensive prayer, and God's leading through years of hard work finally bore blessed fruit.

Church Dedications

In the city of Lvov, near the Polish border, where we met N. A. Zhukaluk and A. N. Kolodyi, among others, we participated in the dedication of the greatly enlarged and redecorated church. Wilson preached the dedicatory sermon, and the program included several musical presentations, testimonies, and a history of the church. The meeting began at 11:00 a.m. and lasted until 4:00 p.m. without a break! Since the 600 seats could not hold the 2,000 who came, a greater part of the audience stood, both inside and outside the church. But no one left early. Many of those fortunate enough to get seats took turns with some who were standing.

Before the church building in Lvov was rebuilt and expanded, three denominations shared it: Baptists, Pentecostals, and Seventh-day Adventists. Now the Pentecostals, with a membership of 1,500, have moved into their own church building on the outskirts of the city. At present the Baptists, with 800 members, and the Seventh-day Adventists, with 350, share the building. Members from both groups contributed a total of 125,000 rubles in cash (one ruble equals approximately US$1.40), and most of the work was voluntary. Since the Adventist membership is about half that of the Baptists, the Baptists contributed two thirds of the expenses and the Adventists one third.

Every workday, from 40 to 50 volunteers from both denominations came to work on the building. The two groups alternated weeks for preparing the food for the workers. The Baptists agreed not to serve pork or anything else against the Adventists' dietary principles. The cooperation went without a hitch. Now each denomination uses the building on specified days. The Baptists worship on Sundays and Wednesdays and the Adventists on Saturdays and Tuesdays. When the two churches are able to buy land and fund the projects, they plan to build their own churches. In the meantime the present unique arrangement functions remarkably well.

The Seventh-day Adventists in Frunze, in the Republic of Kirghizia, also enlarged their church building. When we had visited there four years previously the building seated only about 100 people, but now it can seat 300.

During our visit to this city, only a few hundred miles from China, about 600 people crowded into the building. There we saw a practical novelty that churches in the West ought to copy: a four-sided electronic signboard in the center of the auditorium displayed the numbers of the hymns to be sung. By moving three hands on a little mechanism, the church elder changed the numbers as needed.

Volunteers had done most of the work on this building, and an electrical engineer had taken care of the wiring. He also had built an electric heater into the baptistry in the churchyard.

Many of the members here speak German. They are descended from early settlers in the Volga area. Some churches still preach the sermon in both the Russian and German languages. Recently a shipment of several hundred German Bibles arrived, and this enabled most Adventist families that needed a German Bible to have one.

Wide Spectrum of People

What kinds of people belong to the Seventh-day Adventist Church in the Soviet Union? Are they mostly elderly? Are there youth among churchgoers? What kinds of jobs do they hold? These are some of the questions members in the West ask.

My impression is that Adventists represent most kinds of trades and professions. I know engineers, medical doctors, dentists, teachers, nurses, workers from collective farms, photographers, carpenters, housewives, and factory workers—in fact, the whole spectrum of occupations.

The fact that practically no unemployment exists in the Soviet Union impresses visitors from Western countries. Rather, there is a lack of workers. For this reason, Seventh-day Adventists usually do not confront great problems in finding jobs that allow them to worship on Sabbaths. The introduction of a five-day workweek also contributed to this. At present the Sabbath work problem does not seem much more difficult than in most other countries.

The matter of students and Sabbath classes still creates problems for Adventist young people. Although many factories observe a five-day week, educational institutions still follow a six-day program. Most teachers and educational authorities are loath to let Adventist children have Sabbath off, partly because it creates misunderstandings with other families. Since many adults have Saturdays off from their jobs, they would also like their children free from school so the whole family could go on weekend trips or go to their *dacha* (vacation cabin). If teachers released the children of Sabbathkeeping parents on Saturdays, other parents denied the same privilege would get upset.

Robert Pierson once discussed this problem with one of the officials. The official reminded us that children are not baptized members of the Seventh-day Adventist Church (the law does not permit church membership under 18 years of age), and the parents therefore should not expect them to follow their practices. They must wait until they can decide for themselves. In reply, Pierson simply quoted the fourth commandment, which clearly spells out parental responsibility for minors. This discussion helped to open the eyes of the official to a better understanding of the parents' dilemma.

The great numbers of young people who attend church always impressed us. In some places, such as Moscow, elderly persons predominate in the congregations, but in the provinces more young people attend. The people love music, and the youth eagerly take part in choirs and orchestras. I have not visited a single church that did not have a musical group or two to brighten and bless the congregation. On his first visit to the United States N. A. Zhukaluk commented on his surprise at not finding more and larger choirs and orchestras performing in Adventist churches.

But not only the young people impress visitors. The sight of consecrated elderly Christians actually testifies to a greater miracle than does that of converted young people. Remember

AIR-9

that the Communist revolution took place in 1917. This means that a lifelong exposure to atheist propaganda has failed to convince these senior citizens. It actually accomplished the opposite of what it intended. Atheist teaching deluged them in schools, in children's organizations, in youth groups, in newspapers, magazines, books and posters, in films and on radio and, during the last several decades, on television. Yet, they chose the Christian faith. Therefore these older Christians constitute one of the strongest witnesses to the power of the gospel. Their experience confirms the old truth expressed so well by Augustine: "You have created us to yourself, O God, and the human heart is restless until it finds rest in you."

In the following chapter I will give an overview of the influence of religion in Russia today.

15 Science Cannot Replace Religion

Every time I arrive in Moscow—and the number of visits during the past 16 years, up to and including 1985, adds up to more than a few—several sights never fail to impress me. One is the metro, or subway. For a fare of five kopecks, about 7 cents, one can travel in any direction anywhere on the system, which crisscrosses the great metropolis. Although the system is not new—it opened in 1935—it is clean, quiet, safe, and fast. On certain stretches the trains attain speeds of up to 60 miles per hour, and during rush hours the trains arrive at the stations at intervals of 80 seconds.

The beauty of the stations stuns the visitor. Some of them look like veritable palaces, with marble walls, sculptures, and murals. Sparkling chandeliers or indirect lighting keep them well illuminated. Stained-glass, back-lit panels brighten the central halls. Probably no other metro system in the world measures up to this one for beauty, speed, and efficiency. The Mayakouskaya Station earned a gold medal at the World Exhibition in New York.

Another place where something interesting takes place continually is Red Square. The Russian word for *red* also means "fair" or "beautiful." Every hour a crowd gathers at the entrance of the Lenin Mausoleum to watch the changing of the guard. Two minutes and 45 seconds before the hour strikes, an officer and two soldiers emerge from the Spasskaya Tower in the Kremlin Wall. They march exactly 340 steps, no more, no less. The moment they halt at the doors of the mausoleum, the chimes from the Kremlin announce the beginning of a new hour, and the changing of the guard takes place. Only careful planning of every move and thorough advance practice can result in such a high degree of perfection as the soldiers demonstrate here. When the two soldiers reach their destination, one on each side of the entrance, they stand motionless, almost like wax figures, for one hour.

Countless numbers of people pass the guards to enter the polished red granite and black labradorite tomb. In silence and awe they file slowly past Lenin's embalmed body. David Shipler, of the New York *Times,* who lived in Moscow for two years, mentions a woman who crossed herself as she came into view of the body. Former Yugoslav Vice President Milovan Djilas wrote: "As we ascended into the mausoleum, I saw how simple women in shawls were crossing themselves as though approaching the reliquary of a saint." [1] These may have been isolated instances, but they illustrate the atmosphere of solemnity, almost religious in its intensity, that pervades the mausoleum. One wonders what the founder of modern Communism and promoter of atheism, who termed religion "the opium of the people," would say if he knew that he himself had become a kind of saint.

Museums and exhibitions abound. Their great number and variety make it possible to find something of interest for every taste, whether it be architecture, art, ancient or modern history, science, agriculture, engineering, or religion. In visiting the famous art galleries and Orthodox churches, some of which now house museums, one fact stood out. Even an atheist state cannot hide the Christian religion and its message. Unwittingly, and perhaps not realizing the full effect of its efforts, the state may even awaken religious thoughts in the minds of its people.

The Tretyakov Art Gallery illustrates this. It was already famous in Lenin's time and he loved this treasure house of art. His widow, Nadezhda Krupskaya, writes that when he lived abroad Lenin would borrow a catalogue of the gallery from his friends and "would sit engrossed in it." Today a long line of people usually waits to enter, and those who plan to visit should obtain tickets early in the day. Among its outstanding masterpieces is a huge canvas that hangs in one of its central halls. This painting, by Aleksandr Ivanov, bears the title *The Appearance of Christ to the People*. It shows John the Baptist surrounded by people of all classes, especially the sick and the poor. Evidently they seek help, physical healing, and satisfaction for the longings of their hearts. John points to the solution: the Saviour, Jesus Christ. All the main lines in the picture lead to Him. Every person in the magnificent painting deserves study, but the others seem insignificant when compared to the One whose face is lighted by love, compassion, and strength. The masterpiece preaches its silent sermon to the millions of Russians and foreigners who, caught by its drawing power, stop to ponder its message.

Such art speaks a language that needs no translation. It demonstrates the old truth that one picture is worth a thousand words.

Silent Witnesses

Other silent witnesses to the Christian religion are the old Russian churches, both those open for services and those now used as museums. They stand right in the very heart of Communism. Inside the Kremlin walls one finds the unpretentious yellow Senate building, built by Catherine the Great in the eighteenth century. On its third floor it houses the Council of Ministers, the nerve center of Soviet government and world Communism. The white marble Palace of Congress also stands within the Kremlin walls. Here one becomes conscious of the many languages spoken in the Soviet Union. In the grand hall of the palace, 6,000 people can hear a speech simultaneously translated into 29 languages by the use of electronic equipment. Next neighbors to these supreme centers of Soviet power, four masterfully restored cathedrals dominate the scene. More than a dozen gilded cupolas reflect the sunlight. The names of the cathedrals, such as the Cathedral of the Twelve Apostles, refer to Bible events and characters, and they fill an important place in Russian history. The weddings and christenings of the czars took place in the Cathedral of the Annunciation, their coronations in the Cathedral of the Assumption, and their burials in the Cathedral of the Archangel Michael.

The typical onion-shaped domes or cupolas have different symbolic meanings. One writer states that when Ivan the Terrible built St. Basil's Cathedral in Red Square, each of the multicolored and different shaped cupolas commemorated a separate victory he had won over the Tatars. Another writer suggests that St. Basil's cupolas represent the diverse cultures of Asia, that they express the conviction that Russia had a mission to take the light of the gospel to Asiatic peoples. When we visited the orthodox Church Center of Zagorsk, 40 miles from Moscow, we heard another explanation. Noticing that five domes crown most old churches, I asked one of the teachers at the Academy of Higher Theological Learning about their symbolic meaning. "The four smaller ones represent the four gospel writers, Matthew, Mark, Luke, and John. The central one represents Jesus Christ,'' he answered.

Each dome is topped by that universal symbol of Christianity, a cross. An interesting comment on the meaning of the Christian symbol appeared in the official atheist magazine, *Science and Religion*. The editors printed a letter from a 33-year-old woman. In it she said she knew nothing about God but still she wore a crucifix as a symbol of the invincibility of the Russian people. "Our people went at their enemies with the cross, and won. A mother would see her son off to war, and bless him with a cross. . . . I see it as a powerful force which can repel any evil. In the cross lies the history of the Russian people.'' [2] The editors replied that the cross is not a Russian symbol but a purely religious one. Her letter must have touched a point affecting many readers; otherwise it would not have been published and repudiated.

An unending stream of tourists from all over the world and from every corner of the Soviet Union reflects on the impact of these monumental reminders of religious faith and life. Paintings dating back to the eleventh century cover the inside walls and pillars. As the people gaze at the pictures of Christ, the virgin Mary, the archangel Gabriel, and scenes from the Bible, they must feel the influence of these masterpieces.

Russian icons proliferate in churches, museums, and private homes. Artists created them, the church blessed them, and they became a focal point for religious veneration. For hundreds of years the church considered the icons an aid to the worshiper in making his prayer heard. They became "windows to God." The most famous and revered depicts Jesus and Mary and bears the name *Virgin of Vladimir* or *Our Lady of Kazan*. The last refers to the battle of Kazan, where the icon reportedly performed a miracle, saving Russia from the Tatars. Orthodox families used to place an icon in a "beautiful corner" of their homes, often on a shelf covered with an embroidered white scarf. When entering the room, family members bowed toward the "beautiful corner" as a gesture of respect.

Religion and Science

The scientific triumph on October 4, 1957, when the Soviets sent the first man-made satellite into space, surprised and shocked the world. The Sputnik age had begun. Only a month later they launched *Sputnik II*. It carried the first living creature into orbit, a dog named Laika, and the Soviets indicated that a man might follow soon. This happened on April 12, 1961, when Yuri Alekseyevich Gagarin rocketed into orbit. He circled the earth once, spending 108 minutes in space.

Of course, these exploits excited the Soviet people and their leaders. The space exhibits in Moscow attract great interest. In the north section of Moscow is the U.S.S.R. Exhibition of

135

Economic Achievements. Its buildings and parks cover 500 acres, and, among other things, it depicts Soviet technology used in these first space exploits. Visitors can see a replica of the half-ton *Sputnik II,* showing the dog Laika's position in it, and the world's first spaceship, *Vostok I,* manned by Gagarin.

Just outside the gate to the exhibition stands an impressive 328-foot-tall obelisk, topped by a rocket. It symbolizes the Soviets' leading role in the first conquests of space. The 200-ton monument is made of titanium, a bright metal that does not tarnish with time. The pedestal of the obelisk encloses a theater where spectators may observe the moon, stars, planets, and the earth as seen from space by the cosmonauts.

Atheists use these scientific triumphs to direct propaganda against religion. Proudly they proclaim that modern science proves religion to be only a myth. When science demonstrates that man can now do what people once thought only God could, man will no longer feel the need for Him. I noted in a former Catholic cathedral, which is now a museum, how they feature space science as a contrast to and replacement for religious ideas. And Premier Khrushchev's statement is well known: "Russian cosmonauts have gone into the heavens far higher than any others; did they see God while they were up there? No, of course not, for there is no God!" [3]

The launching of the Sputniks revived the old claim that "Soviet man has driven the gods from out of the sky." One Communist paper quoted the director of the Moscow planetarium as saying: "Now that the first two sputniks have appeared in the cosmos, it is possible to say that we have visited heaven. . . . We have been where the eyes of the believer are directed with religious awe." [4] A typical antireligious poster, issued by the state atheist organization Znanie ("knowledge") and currently in use dwells on the same theme. In the upper part it shows an old grandmother pointing her daughter to an icon and admonishing: "Don't cross the threshold without God!" The lower and dominating part of the poster shows the daughter watching, via television, Sputnik speeding toward the stars. Smiling, she throws the icon away.

The believers' reaction to this kind of propaganda disappoints the atheists. A typical story in Christian circles tells of a teacher who asked his students why the astronauts saw no angels and no God in outer space. One boy answered, "They probably did not go high enough!" *Izvestiya,* the government daily newspaper, which enjoys an enormous circulation, once quoted Madame Krupskaya, Lenin's widow, showing how easily antireligious propaganda misfires. She told of a Moscow workman who, in leaving the planetarium, said, "Well, well, who would have believed how wisely God has organized the world!" [5] His statement illustrates what Abraham Lincoln once said: "I can see how it might be possible for a man to look down upon the earth and be an atheist, but I cannot conceive how he could look up into the heavens and say there is no God." [6]

Faith Gives Meaning to Life

Nobody knows for sure how many people in the Soviet Union believe in God. I once asked Archimandrite Georgy in the Orthodox Church Center at Zagorsk if he knew how many adherents the Orthodox Church has in the country. He answered, "Religion is a private matter, and we have no definite figures. When we baptize we don't even ask the full name of the candidate, only the Christian name." But he and other church officials expressed the view that interest in religion is growing. Some estimate that from 30 to 50 million profess the Russian Orthodox faith, although many of them do not strictly follow all its precepts, such as fast days and church rituals. The small Protestant denominations do register their members. After his first visits to the U.S.S.R., Billy Graham estimated that about 100 million people believe in God.[7] Of these approximately half are Christians and the other half Muslims.

Religion does not necessarily express itself in church membership and the performance of religious rites. Religion consists of active faith in God, prayers, and pious thoughts. Nobody can look into the depths of every human soul in the Soviet Union and determine that person's degree of dedication to God. But that widespread commitment and faith exist is evident from many sources. A leading Soviet pedagogical journal printed a revealing letter from a university-trained woman teacher. The fact that the editors published it and found it necessary to write a long refutation reveals that it must represent an attitude on the part of many. She wrote:

"I have recently read in the papers how various people have broken with religion. . . . Why may I not write and publish in a journal about how I came to Christianity, in what way and for what motives I have come to believe in God? . . . I felt the need for answers to these questions: Whence came human suffering? Why does man live? and What does true happiness consist of? . . . I thoroughly worked through Indian philosophy, the gospels, etc. And as a result of all this I came to the conclusion that only religion, faith in Christ, gives meaning to human life, gives warmth and light to the human soul. Science, then, should be subordinate to religion, because when unchecked by religion as now, it works toward destruction." [8]

That religion is not limited to "old women going to church," as tourist guides often state, Soviet sources verify. An article printed in *Izvestiya* under the title "What Is Happening to Religion, Its Rituals and Traditions?" by Ye. Filimonov, Ph.D., begins by stating that the majority of Soviet citizens are not influenced by religion. The article continues:

"On the other hand, there are still not a few people who are unable, for one reason or another, to master a scientific-materialist worldview, who pay their respects in various ways to religious confessions and who observe religious rituals and traditions. And in Orthodox and other churches, especially in the prayer houses of Baptists, Adventists, and Pentecostals, one may see young people at the services. It has become 'stylish' to marry in church, baptize one's children, and to wear a cross."

Pravda, probably the largest daily newspaper in the world, with a circulation of more than 7 million, is just as open. An article entitled "Atheism Is the Struggle for Man" contained the following:

"Today it is essential to reexamine the traditional concept of a believer. The mass of believers are people who, as a rule, are literate, engaged in socially productive work, and interested in both domestic and international affairs as well as information about science. For a significant number, the tendency toward a rational basis for their faith . . . is characteristic." [9] And Alexei Bichkov, general secretary of the All-Union Council of Evangelical Christians-Baptists, states: "Agnostics, intellectuals, scientists, and other university graduates are among those becoming devoted followers of Christ." [10]

Nobody can really question this fact: religion is far from being eradicated in Soviet minds.

16

Russian Adventists
Welcome Visitors

A long-cherished dream became reality when my wife and I spent some unforgettable days with Adventists in the heart of western Siberia in the summer of 1983. This was a prelude to our visit to eastern Siberia a couple years later.

To most of us who live in the West, the name Siberia brings to the mind's eye pictures of frozen wastes and a harsh climate that make life a struggle. This probably comes from the many stories we have heard about people who were considered undesirable being banished to Siberia.

What would we find out about religious life in such a place? Can people attend meetings? Do the church members have Bibles? Do young people join in the worships? We found the answers to these and many other questions and will try to report what we saw, heard, and experienced. But a lot of things happened on our trip before we arrived there.

First we went to the city of Tula, south of Moscow, where earlier we had seen a church under construction. Now we viewed the finished building, but even more attractive than the church was the number of fine young people attending the meetings. They welcomed us with a lively musical and historical program. A young scholar recited key episodes from Russian church history, interspersed with numbers from musical groups. Similar to what happened in Tallinn on a previous visit, the program climaxed with an outstanding choir performance of Handel's "Hallelujah Chorus." As in other parts of the world, the audience stood during this number. Everyone in the choir dressed attractively. The ladies wore floor-length peach-colored dresses, and the men wore black suits with white shirts and black bow ties.

Site of Fierce Battle

Our itinerary included the city of Volgograd, formerly Stalingrad. During World War II this city was the site of one of the fiercest battles ever fought. In the summer of 1942 Nazi troups stormed the city in an effort to mop up the Caucasus and capture Moscow. For five and one-half months the battle raged. In its various stages it involved more than 2 million men, 2,000 tanks, and 2,000 planes.

Survivors remember Mamayev Heights, on the outskirts of the city, which changed hands several times. The blood of fallen soldiers soaked the earth. Today a gigantic 150-foot monument crowns the hilltop. Also impressive is a panorama of the battle, housed in a huge circular building. From a high platform in the center, visitors can view the dramatic scenes. The area between the platform and the painting is covered with weapons, tanks, debris from the battle, and wax figures of fighting soldiers, which blend into the painting on the circular wall. One has the feeling of being in the midst of the battle itself.

Not a single building in the center of the city escaped destruction. During the fighting torrents of burning fuel flowed onto the Volga, making it a river of fire that set all the ships on the water ablaze. The bombardment and house-to-house fighting killed 40,000 civilians and wounded 150,000. By the close of the war only 32,000 remained in the city, which formerly counted a half million inhabitants.

A new city with a population of approximately 1 million has arisen from the ruins of the old. It is sobering to realize that before rebuilding could begin, ammunition experts defused more than one and a half million mines, shells, and bombs.

A few years ago only a handful of Adventists met on Sabbaths in this city. Today approximately 100 people crowd into the simple house of worship. At the time of our visit many more came in from surrounding areas. As everywhere else in the Soviet Union, we received a warm welcome and overwhelming hospitality. We also found a deep interest in the preaching of God's Word. The local pastor scheduled our meeting for 6:00 p.m. Since this was a weekday, I asked why they arranged it to begin so early. He answered, ''We want the meeting to begin early so it can last a long time!''

The area representative for the Ministry of Religious Affairs met us on our arrival and assisted us in every possible way during our visit. He personally arranged for an English-speaking guide, who showed us some of the memorials of the big battles fought in 1942. The bloody encounters ended with a decisive but costly victory for the Soviet Army. It actually turned the tide of World War II in the East. It is estimated that 200,000 German soldiers perished here and more than 90,000 were taken prisoner.

The stark realities of war come to life in such a place, especially the unbelievable sufferings and losses of the Soviet Union. Of the 45 million casualities of World War II (dead, wounded, and missing), 20 million were citizens of this one country. An unknown number, undoubtedly running into many thousands, died in concentration camps. Others lost their lives in battles and bombings. Starvation and the shelling of cities took a large toll. Hardly a family in the Soviet Union escaped without the loss of one or more of its loved ones.

The official from the Ministry of Religous Affairs in Volgograd attended our meeting in the church and the luncheon that followed. I spoke about Christ's first miracle, turning water into wine. Afterward he confided; ''I am not a Christian, but I agree with everything you said except when you stated the wine served at the wedding feast in Cana did not contain alcohol!'' He arranged for me to visit Archbishop Pimen in the Kazan

143

Mother of God church, which is open for services.

When we arrived we saw hundreds of people press around the archbishop to receive his blessing as he placed his hands on their heads. After the service we spent a profitable evening and shared a supper with the archbishop and a number of Orthodox priests. They informed us that parents come every day with their babies to be baptized. The church officially teaches baptism by immersion, but for the sake of convenience the ceremony usually consists of sprinkling a little water on babies' heads. In some churches, however, we noted baptistries in the floor deep enough for the priests to baptize adults by immersion.

Visiting Siberia

Although travel plans allowed for arrival in western Siberia's cultural capital, Novosibirsk, with time to spare before our Sabbath appointments, unavoidable delays caused a drastic change in our schedule. When the plane touched down on Siberian asphalt, my watch read 4:00 a.m. on Sabbath morning by Moscow time. But by local time it was 8:00 a.m. This meant we would have no sleep at all before a full day with Adventists in Novosibirsk. It seemed that we had time only to rush to the hotel to change our clothes.

We did not expect any breakfast at all, so it came as a pleasant surprise when the pastor's wife, Mrs. Himinetz, and her helpers brought a delicious breakfast of bread, butter, jam, milk, fruit, cakes, honey, and cheese to our hotel room. They even brought a tablecloth, napkins, and hot chocolate in a thermos.

Although we had slept very little during the previous 24 hours, the problems of our travel to this distant place did not compare to the hardships our pioneer workers suffered as they began the work here or visited groups of believers later. In 1908 a Russian-born minister, K. A. Reifschneider, with headquarters in Omsk, Siberia, traveled 2,000 miles, largely in horse-drawn sledges. H. J. Loebsack traveled 28,000 miles in

1925. He journeyed most of the time under comparatively primitive conditions by train, boat, wagon, and in winter, by sledge. These itineraries allowed little time for sleep and rest. We sympathize when he writes:

"Often I feel so tired that I would like to lie flat on the floor to rest a few weeks, and relax entirely, but the time is not yet. My only hope is in the fulfillment of Revelation 14:13: 'Blessed are the dead which die in the Lord from henceforth: Yea, saith the Spirit, that they may rest from their labours; and their works do follow them.' And I believe that even then I shall toil on for some 25 or 50 years more, to make up for what I missed while on earth. O, how I love to continue in this good work!"

After one of his long and tiresome trips, sickness forced Loebsack to stay in bed. He commented on his fate in these words: "The doctor whom I usually consult when death seems imminent, has sentenced me to two weeks' rest in my home. Very reluctantly was I compelled to submit to this command. It is as I have always said, if I cannot speak, I write; and if I cannot write, I meditate, and make poetry; if I cannot make poetry, I pray; if I cannot pray, I rest; and then the effect of my work will have to continue of itself."

With a touch of humor he added: "I have often been sick, but by the grace of God I have not yet died once." Then he quotes from Psalm 118:17, 18: "I shall not die, but live, and declare the works of the Lord. The Lord hath chastened me sore: but he hath not given me over unto death." [1]

Even the visiting brethren from the General Conference had their share of unusual travel adventures. L. R. Conradi reported on one of his visits to Russia: "I have spent 15 nights on car [train] and steamer as travel in some parts is very slow. Besides, I have made some 200 miles by wagon; but thus far I have been unharmed and with my good fur slept in the third class as well or better than many in the first class."

W. A. Spicer, secretary and later president of the General Conference, also visited Russia. At that time danger threatened foreigners who traveled there. A woman told his daughter, Helen Menkel, this story: "My husband's father lived in Russia, and when your father came to visit he was asked to take him around to the different churches. They were afraid something would happen to him if the authorities saw that he was a stranger. They decided on a plan. They filled a cart with hay and put him under the hay and covered him up. That is the way he traveled from church to church." [2]

Taking into account these experiences of my predecessors, we had absolutely no reason to complain!

New Siberian Church Dedicated

After a quick breakfast, District Leader D. A. Grenz took us by taxi to the meetings. As we neared the church, however, we noted that the brethren smilingly said something to the driver, and I got the definite impression the car circled a few blocks. Later we found out why. The church leaders had arranged for a special reception outside the church at a certain time, and everything needed to be ready. They did not want us to arrive too early!

When we turned the last corner and stopped in front of the church, an unforgettable sight greeted us. Hundreds of Siberian believers crowded around the building. In the center a young couple in colorful national costume walked toward us with the traditional round loaf of bread and a little dish of salt. These symbolize welcome and hospitality. Someone told us the custom stems from the old days when people living out in the country left their houses to work in the fields. In case a hungry stranger should happen by, they left bread and salt on the table so he could serve himself. We could not help being touched by such a lovely welcome, and immediately we felt close to these friendly people in the middle of Siberia. All thought of sleep disappeared from our minds.

The church to be dedicated on this Sabbath seated about 300 and was constructed entirely by Adventist volunteer labor.

146

Visitors from churches in Omsk, Novokuznetsk, Tomsk, Irkutsk, Bijsk, Semipalatinsk, Tastaminagorsk, and other places in Siberia joined in the celebration. The hospitality of the Novosibirsk church was striking. Everyone shared in the noon meal. The men set up long tables in the churchyard and the women served an abundance of delicious food.

Soviet demographers estimate that the average age of the 23 million people living in Siberia is only 26. This preponderance of young people in the population is reflected in the churches. They seemed a happy, tightly knit group, eager to take part in church functions, especially the instrumental and choir groups. Repeatedly I marveled at their willingness to stand for hours during services because all the seats were taken. We noted here also that quite a few Adventists own Bibles and take them to Bible study and worship services.

Time did not permit us to see many of the sights in and around Novosibirsk, a city of 1.3 million people. But we did take advantage of the opportunity to visit Akademgorok, a huge scientific research center located 19 miles outside the city. Here 21 academic institutes work side by side and in close cooperation with other scientific centers throughout the region.

Siberia's abundance of natural resources in the form of coal, oil, minerals, timber, and hydropower is the reason Soviet journals make statements such as "Russia's might will depend on Siberia." One journal goes so far as to state, "Siberia delights, lures, frightens, and stuns with its beauty. Anyone who is not aware of this expansive land knows nothing about the future of our planet."

The extremes of temperature varying from tropical heat in the short summer to -75° F in winter, produces unique conditions. Of Siberia's 5 million square miles, one third is tundra, four fifths of which is permanently frozen. This causes special difficulties for agriculture and the construction of buildings. Scientists at Akademgorok, in cooperation with local industry, try hard to find solutions to these and other problems.

The immense coal reserves await mining. One field alone contains 450 billion tons. A scientist visiting Krasnoyarsk found that a village near Divnogorsk stands on top of a coal seam. The cellars of the houses are actually minature coal pits. The owners climb down into them and dig out the coal they need for their stoves.

Growth in Sochi

The last part of our journey took us to the subtropical Caucasus in the south, to the cities of Suchumi and Sochi by the Black Sea. We spoke to large audiences eager for fellowship and the message from God's Word.

Under the leadership of Pastor Sitnik, Adventists in Sochi had rebuilt, enlarged, and redecorated their church. Again we participated in a dedication service. For the first time in the history of the Adventist Church in the U.S.S.R., an archpriest of the Russian Orthodox Church attended the dedication. At the close he expressed his appreciation for the service and added the wish that the church would grow in spiritual strength and in membership.

As I looked at the packed church during the dedication, I could not help thinking of the start of the work here. Loebsack told the General Conference session in 1909: ''It is also interesting to note the beginning of the work in Sotschy, which is a health resort on the Baltic Sea. During the time of the insurrection, the people surrounded the house of a brother who lived there and wanted to kill him. He hid a few days among the mountains, but he finally thought, 'I will be more safe in the hands of the police than among these people who wish to do me harm.' So he took his Bible and went to the marketplace and there he spoke to the people. Through this, the better classes of the people stood up for him, and they wanted to go against his enemies.

''All of them are arrested. His literature, among which was a Sabbath-school lesson quarterly about our relation to the

148

government, was sent to the government with the minutes of this meeting. As a result of this Sabbath-school lesson about our relation to the authorities, he received his freedom, and his enemies were kept in prison. Since then we have been able to establish a Russian church in this place." [3]

The members faithfully witnessed of their newfound faith. When, for instance, J. T. Boetcher visited a lighthouse near Sochi, on the shores of the Black Sea, he discovered their footprints. He writes: "As I went up into the lighthouse and entered, the director, who was an officer who had been wounded in the Russian-Japanese war, asked whether I was a representative of the Advent doctrine for the Caucasus or for the whole of Russia. Although secretly and inwardly he leaned more to the Muhammadans than to the Christians, yet he could recognize the utility of such a society as ours and could admire our wonderful organization throughout the whole world."

Boetcher then went upstairs in the lighthouse. He describes what he saw: on the table "there lay an open Bible and a volume of our Russian paper, and also an open Sabbath school lesson pamphlet. The watchman was an Orthodox Greek Christian; and during the night he sought for spiritual light as he allowed the light of the lighthouse to shine out over the dark waters." [4]

Tourists from all over the world visit Sochi every year. As is true elsewhere in the Soviet Union, wherever Adventist churches are located the members welcome visitors in their services. Even though they cannot understand the language, they can enjoy the music and feel the love of the people reflected in their beaming faces and warm handshakes. It is a never-to-be-forgotten experience.

149

17 "The Weakness of God Is Stronger Than Man"

God's guiding hand prepared early for His message to enter Russia, a land that seemed closed. One hundred years before the Seventh-day Adventist Church organization was established in the United States of America, Catherine the Great invited to her country those who became the forerunners of Russian Adventists. When the right time came He led them to America and Canada, where some of them found the three angels' messages. Then the most unlikely missionary, a poor old man, supported by no one and discouraged by many, with poor eyesight and handicapped in his speech, volunteered to return to Russia and share his newfound light. He proved that "the foolishness of God is wiser than men, and the weakness of God is stronger than men" and demonstrated that "God chose what is weak in the world to shame the strong" (1 Cor. 1:25, 27, RSV). It sounds paradoxical, but his weakness made an impossible task possible!

In the years that followed, it sometimes looked as though the seed he and other early pioneers sowed would die. But God, the only One able to do so, "gave the growth" (1 Cor. 3:7, RSV).

Adventist leaders in Russia used another metaphor, but it tells the same story: "We have the firm conviction that it is not due to our own understanding and strength that the little boat of faith that holds God's people has come safely through the storms. It has been solely a result of the power of the Holy

Spirit, which will continue to lead us in the gospel work.''*

Not only did the church survive, but it experienced a steady growth through the years, as the following membership figures show:

1910	3,952
1915	5,236
1920	8,200
1925	12,434
1930	13,709
1935	No report
1940	16,513
1945	No report
1950	21,611
1951-1981	No report
1982	30,604
1985 (June)	31,305

Some recent gatherings showed that the optimism of the early leaders was not unfounded. They believed, as did the apostle Paul, that "in due season we shall reap, if we do not lose heart" (Gal. 6:9, RSV).

Unique Gatherings

One of these gatherings took place in the Ukraine in 1984 in Vinnitsa, a city where no one from Adventist headquarters had visited before. The Ukrainian leader, N. A. Zhukaluk, showed us a little private house where he and his wife led a Bible study group and organized the first small church many years ago. Soon the growing membership forced a move into a larger hall. It did not stop there, for the swelling church needed more space. Again the authorities permitted another doubling of the church's seating capacity. Here we met during our visit, and the overflowing crowds underlined the need for a fourth doubling of space. The associate Ukrainian leader, V. I. Prolinski, assured us that the permission to expand would soon be granted.

When we drove from the hotel to the church a large number of "Adventist cars" followed our two taxis, forming a long motorcade. The police gave special permission for this impressive procession of cars to drive through avenues not usually open to that kind of traffic. To mark it as a special arrangement, the police ordered all the cars participating to turn on their headlights. The quarter million people in the city certainly noticed that Adventists had come to town!

A friendly Baptist pastor showed us a new 900-seat church under construction. He invited me to speak at the dedication, scheduled for a short time in the future. Since we did not intend to stay that long, he invited me to speak in the present church the following Sunday morning. Again an event to remember. A well-trained mandolin ensemble and a beautiful choir enhanced the service. From the pulpit I looked into several hundred friendly faces of people sitting and standing all over the auditorium. On Sundays the Baptists held several services to accommodate all the worshipers. Who can forget such memories? And even more thrilling experiences brightened this same visit.

The Phillips translation of the Bible terms one Sabbath in Christ's time as having been "particularly important"; another translation calls it "very special (John 19:31, TLB). For thousands of Seventh-day Adventists in the U.S.S.R., the Sabbath of June 2, 1984, also stands out as very special, although for different reasons.

People in Western countries who usually hear of Soviet restrictions on religious gatherings would hardly have believed their eyes if they had seen what happened in the city of Chernovtsy that Sabbath morning. Believers streamed in from all directions, walking, cycling, or arriving in buses and hundreds of private cars. Some flew long distances by Aeroflot Airlines and other came by train. By the time we sang the opening hymn, N. A. Zhukaluk estimated, 3,500 persons were present. This made it the largest meeting ever held in the 100-year history of Adventists in Russia.

In the seven years since our earlier visit, the congregation in Chernovtsy had worked hard and expanded the church's seating capacity from 400 to 800. This, of course, far from satisfied the needs of such a crowd. The brethren knew solutions. Following the practice of the Orthodox Church, where all stand during the services, they carried out most of the chairs and benches and placed them around the outside of the building. This gave standing room for hundreds more inside, and the large crowd outside had some seating. They listened through loudspeakers. Fortunately, beautiful weather aided the arrangements.

One amusing detail lingers in my mind. Four intelligent young people decided that the shutter in the ceiling, which opened for ventilation, might serve another purpose as well. They searched until they found access to the attic, crawled on all fours over to the vent, and during the service their happy faces appeared in the little opening. The audience probably suffered for want of air, since the young people blocked the opening, but these lucky ones enjoyed a grandstand view of everything going on beneath them!

The preaching of the Word, of course, was central to the service, but lots of other things happened. Brass bands played and beautiful Russian music was presented by choirs, soloists, duets, and quartets. Violins and electric guitars were not lacking, either. Besides, just meeting and associating with all the fellow believers made it a special Sabbath indeed.

No one can measure religious faith, but my impression is that in the Soviet Union a deep and heartfelt spirituality fills both young and old. They enjoy their faith and long for God's people to be completely united and ready for the realization of the blessed hope.

References

Chapter 2

*Ellen G. White, *Maranatha: The Lord is Coming* (Washington, D.C.: Review and Herald Pub. Assn., 1976), p. 128.

Chapter 3

¹ Alf Lohne, "I Preached to Thousands in the Soviet Union," *Review and Herald,* July 14, 1977.
² Golda Meir, *My Life* (New York: G. P. Putnam's Sons, 1975), p. 252.

Chapter 4

¹ J. C. Wenger, *How Mennonites Came to Be* (Scottdale, Pa: Herald Press, 1977), pp. 41, 42.
² Frank Wall and Ava Wall, *Uncertain Journey* (Washington, D.C.: Review and Herald Pub. Assn., 1974), p. 21.
³ See John Toews, *Czars, Soviets, and Mennonites* (Newton, Kans.: Faith and Life, 1982), p. 3.
⁴ James Billington, *The Icon and the Axe* (New York: Vintage Books, 1970), pp. 223, 224.
⁵ Toews, p. 6.
⁶ See Walter Kolarz, *Religion in the Soviet Union* (New York: St. Martin's Press, 1961), p. 277.
⁷ Wall, pp. 29, 30.
⁸ Paul Aurandt, *Paul Harvey's the Rest of the Story* (Garden City, N.Y.: Doubleday and Co., Inc., 1977), pp. 83, 84.

Chapter 5

[1] Adaline Reimche, "How the German Work Began," *Adventist Review*, Apr. 29, 1982.

[2] *General Conference Bulltin*, 1909, p. 53.

[3] *Ibid*.

[4] *Ibid*.

[5] *Ibid*.

[6] *Ibid*., p. 52.

[7] L. R. Conradi, "The German and Russian Fields," *Review and Herald*, Apr. 4, 1893.

[8] *Ibid*.

Chapter 6

[1] Kurt Bangert, *Advent Echo*, May 1, 1982, pp. 12, 13. See also Conradi, Louis Richard, *Seventh-day Adventist Encyclopedia* (Washington, D.C.: Review and Herald Pub. Assn., 1976), p. 348

[2] William Spicer, *Our Story of Missions* (Mountain View, Calif.: Pacific Press Pub. Assn., 1921), p. 173 (for a more detailed account of Conradi's trip to Russia, see L. R. Conradi, "A Visit to Russia," in *Historical Sketches* [Basle: Imprimerie Polyglotte, 1886], pp. 250-271); *General Conference Bulletin*, 1909, pp. 52-54.

[3] Arthur W. Spalding, *Origin and History of the Seventh-day Adventist Church* (Washington, D.C.: Review and Herald Pub. Assn., 1961, 1962), vol. 2, pp. 232, 233.

[4] Conradi, in *Historical Sketches*, pp. 262, 263.

[5] *Ibid*., p. 263.

[6] *Ibid*., p. 271.

Chapter 7

[1] P. T. Magan, "Russia's Religious Laws," *Review and Herald*, Feb. 17, 1891.

[2] Conradi, "The German and Russian Fields," *Review and Herald*, Apr. 4, 1893.

[3] Quoted in J. N. Andrews and L. R. Conradi, *History of the Sabbath*, 4th ed. (Washington, D.C.: Review and Herald Pub. Assn., 1912), p. 664.

[4] L. R. Conradi, "The German-Russian Mission Field," *Review and Herald*, Dec. 5, 1893.

[5] Jean Zurcher, "John N. Andrews: The Christopher Columbus of

Adventism,'' *Adventist Heritage* 9, No. 1 (1984): 39.

[6] Conradi, ''The German-Russian Mission Field.''

[7] *Ibid.*

[8] *Ibid.*

[9] *Ibid.*

[10] ———, in *Historical Sketches,* pp. 268, 269.

[11] ———, ''Work in Russia,'' *Review and Herald,* May 1, 1888.

[12] M. E. Olsen, *Origin and Progress of the Seventh-day Adventists* (Washington, D.C.: Review and Herald Pub. Assn., 1925), pp. 479, 480; see also John N. Loughborough, *The Great Second Advent Movement* (Washington, D.C.: Review and Herald Pub. Assn., 1909), p. 411.

[13] Spicer, *Our Story of Missions,* p. 177.

[14] *Der Adventbote,* Nov. 1, 1927.

[15] Kolarz, *Religion in the Soviet Union,* p. 323.

[16] *General Conference Bulletin,* 1909, p. 36.

Chapter 8

[1] *General Conference Bulletin,* 1909, p. 52.

[2] *Ibid.*

[3] Spicer, *Our Story of Missions,* p. 179.

[4] *Ibid.,* p. 180.

[5] *Ibid.*

[6] J. T. Boettcher, ''Progress in Russia,'' *Review and Herald,* Nov. 23, 1911.

[7] *Ibid.*

[8] *Ibid.*

[9] *SDA Encyclopedia,* p. 1527.

Chapter 9

[1] *Der Adventbote,* Mar. 1, 1922.

[2] Walter Sawatsky, *Soviet Evangelicals Since World War II* (Scottdale, Pa.: Herald Press, 1945), p. 105.

[3] Matthew Spinka, *The Church and the Russian Revolution* (New York: The Macmillan Company, 1927), p. 105.

[4] *Ibid.,* pp. 141, 142; from V. I. Lenin, *On Rural Poverty* (1903), in Michael Bourdeaux, *Religious Ferment in Russia* (New York: St. Martin's Press, 1968), p. 108; Constitution of the Union of Soviet Socialist Republics (Moscow: Novosti Press Agency Pub. House, 1982), p. 34.

Chapter 10

[1] *Pravda,* 1924, No. 108, quoted in Kolarz, *Religion in the Soviet Union,* p. 288.

[2] Kolarz, p. 288.

[3] K. Petrus, "Religious Communes in the U.S.S.R." (research program on the U.S.S.R., New York), p. 19.

[4] *Der Adventbote,* June 1927, p. 19.

[5] Kolarz, pp. 292, 293.

Chapter 11

[1] Maurice Hindus, Harrison Smith, and Robert Haas, *The Great Offensive* (New York: Random House, 1933), pp. 168, 169.

[2] *Report From the 1924 Congress in Moscow* (translated by Professor Elffers for Elder W. H. Branson from one of the original 5,000 copies printed in Russia; sent to Elders W. A. Spicer and L. J. Shaw, Jan. 21, 1925). Actions of the congress also appear in F. Fedorenko, *Sects, Their Faith and Works* (Moscow: 1965), pp. 186-188.

[3] *Religion in Communist Lands,* 8, No. 3 (Autumn 1980): 214.

[4] *Ibid.,* p. 202.

[5] *General Conference Bulletin,* 1922, p. 267.

[6] *Liberty,* September/October 1985, p. 3. (Italics supplied.)

[7] *Meeting With the Opposition Movement,* July 20-23, 1920, in Friedensau, Germany (printed by the three German unions of Seventh-day Adventists), pp. 37-39.

[8] *Der Adventbote,* No. 7, 1928.

[9] *SDA Encyclopedia,* p. 1531.

Chapter 12

[1] G. Zirat to W. A. Spicer, Nov. 24, 1926.

[2] *Der Adventbote,* Nov. 7, 1926.

[3] *Religion in Communist Lands* 18, No. 3 (Autumn 1980): 202-705.

[4] *Ibid.* (Summer 1977): 91.

[5] *Ibid.,* p. 93.

[6] *Ibid.,* pp. 89, 90, in F. Federenko, *Sects, Their Faith and Works,* p. 291.

Chapter 13

[*] Ellen G. White, *Steps to Christ* (Mountain View, Calif.: Pacific Press Publishing Assn., 1956), pp. 59-61.